I0503317

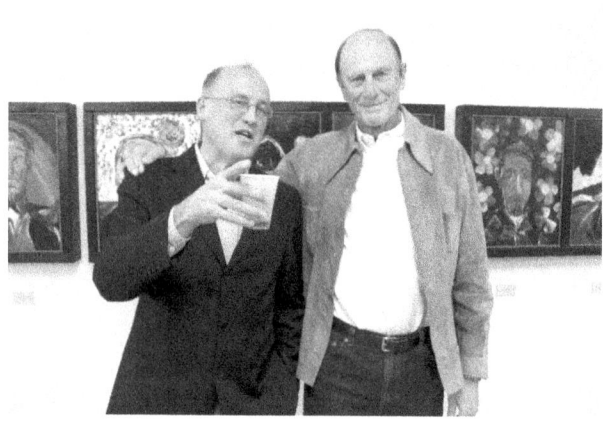

"Just Remember Duckies, Everybody Gets Got"

The quoted title is from a recent David Bowie song, "I'd Rather Be High".

I had a solo exhibitionon American history. Half the show was about my ancestors of Hamilton, NY. The portraits behind me in the photo are five of eleven generations of patronym I researched a couple years ago. I visited each grave but one, from puritan William (far left) to my Grandfather Ronald (not shown). My father and I are still ungot, although he's the better dresser and for that reason alone, should carry on several years longer than me.

The exhibition was a financial failure beyond psychological repair. Some wide receivers in the NFL make a half million dollars a week, and they still drop the ball. And yet even this modern reality would not make my ancestors shudder in their graves, until called by the battle bugle to roll out of them as farm implement wielding zombies to hack frenzied at a culture gone cuckoo-media to the extreme.

Not including dinner for the family, where we dressed all nicely and pretended success like 1954 with a log burning in the restaurant fireplace, my losses were about $400.00. You can tell from the photo that I am not at all worried, because I had just landed a job cooking and washing my own pots and pans at an elder care facility. How was I to know that three weeks later I'd be heckled by a resident during the turkey carving ceremony on Thanksgiving? Drove me to distraction all week. Yesterday I decided that the quest for money via the personal creation of anything is insane. So I quit my job and have officially fallen into the cradling good graces of my darling wife, whom I shall accept full support from until I am got.

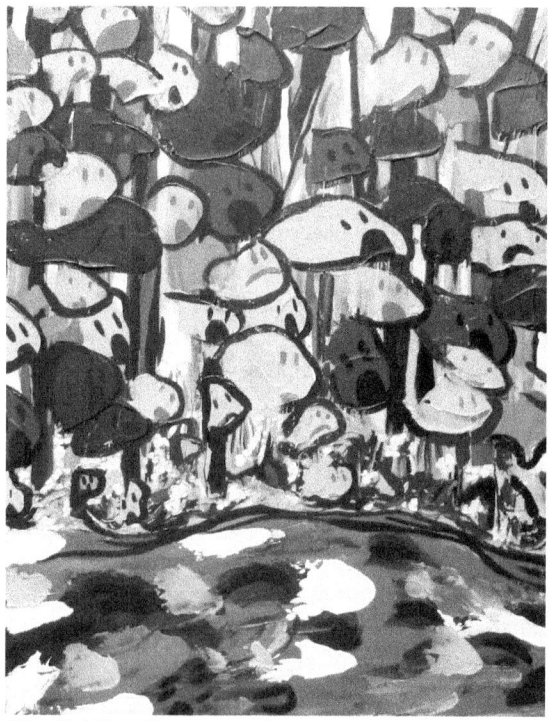

Ghost Fish Float Above Benzene Stream 2015.
Acrylic on canvas, 16 x 20"

A Very Short Story I Wrote Before My Second Cup of Coffee About My Fall From Grace As A Painter

Finally! I have been contractually released from my indentured servitude. I am no longer working for the big guy in the sky. Holiday perks were actually fewer than what I got on any hair shirt day of the week, and I began to dread plain oatmeal served cold in a wood bowl. The constant walking was hell on the feet, and the heart attack trumpet sounding off the frequent Armageddon drills was making me schizophrenic. Enough! I couldn't take it anymore. So I literally got down on my knees and begged Penance Peter the overseer to chisel out my frontal lobe with a rusty fork. As usual, he would have nothing to do with my begging and pleading (I swear he actually gets off on it). So I went over his head to the palace on high, ran fearlessly forward into the blinding light, straight up to the throne of gold blazing and called out demanding my release.

"Why should I let you go?" said the thundering sky surround sound.

I called out, "I want to be a painter—"

"You are."

"...who can sell a pain—"

I woke up standing in a beautiful white gallery with all of my creations hung on a wall. Each one had a red dot stuck under the title, and many tall, thin, young-looking people dressed in black and jewelry, holding drinks, were smiling at me. A silver-haired man approached and shook my hand.

"Hello Ron. I am Larry Beelzebub Gagosian. Welcome to Hell. Do not walk to the door. Do not stop smiling. I have an appointment scheduled later for you with Paul Allen and David Geffen. I want you to talk about nothing but cheese and a dollar that you found on the sidewalk today. Do not sniffle, but stick a finger in your belly button from time to time. You will be a millionaire by midnight."

"Thank you Mr. Gagosian!"

"There's one caveat," he said.

"And what is that?" I asked.

"Every painting from now until you die must have those colorful clouds spread on in exactly the same fashion."

"Do they have to be the same color?"

"Yes, I'm afraid so."

"Same arrangement?"

"No. You may turn them upside down, elongate or compress, and of course you are free to choose any size of canvas we stretch here in Hell."

"It's a deal!" I cried.

"Great. Start talking about cheese…"

The End.

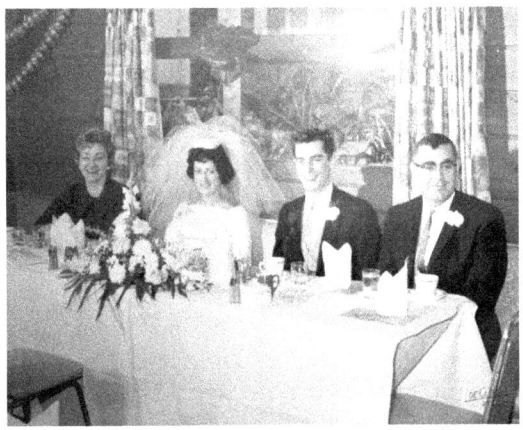

Waxing Nostalgic On Time and Spirit

These are my parents, Keitha and David, on their wedding day. His brother Bill and her sister Toni Marie. I won't be born for five years, yet I already know this place very well in my future dreams. The Seneca Inn. It is the restaurant my grandparents own on route 5, before the time of the great atomization, and the construction of the corporate-friendly, human-hating thoroughfare called the New York State Thruway. The bride cleaned rental cottages since she was eleven. The groom would hitchhike across town to visit with her during courtship. She liked courtship. He liked cars and duck's asses. My grandfather offered to buy Keitha a 1963 Jaguar if she would postpone marriage and go to Cazenovia College where she was accepted. She would have no part in that heartbreaking scheme! After a frozen honeymoon in Gettysburg (the groom's bad idea), they set up housekeeping in a rented pink trailer a few hundred yards up the road from the restaurant.

I have been gorging myself on their memories my whole life, yet am unable to receive any digestive satisfaction. I am not born. I am spirit of Christmases yet to come. In this future I have lived there exists a fullness like the unknown memory I have of the

Seneca Inn, the patrons, the staff, my grandfather who died before I am born to write this... Aunts and uncles will exodus—the two in the photo would be the first in the family to leave Central New York for private and economic reasons. Before that, beyond the call of war, there was only localism. It was life, c'est la vie, and you made of it what you could where you were born. Family was slow and purposeful. Children met and fell in love in high school, and were married. Each could throw a rock to the family home of the other, and monstrosities like Ted Turner had no eternal claim to any living room in the county.

Christmas shopping downtown in shops at the Busy Corner and The Boston Store. Then the settling in of rock n' roll, the village shoe store moves to the shopping center, and then to the mall. My generation born and raised without knowing the joys of liquid lunch, nor the pathetic tales of traveling salesmen. Never the solace of loneliness bolstered by the rock of community trust that welcomes all travelers back to their sense of place.

My painting of the Seneca Inn.

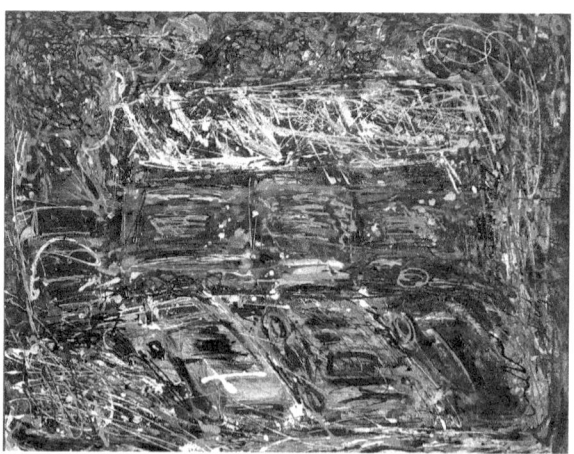

The Seneca Inn 2012. Acrylic on panel board, 48 x 32"

I am still a sojourner in life. I am not home even in this town where I have lived for nearly thirty years, 90 miles from the Seneca Inn. I go back to New Hartford and Utica for a visit and wax nostalgic over a time that never was, but will come again, soon after the Industrial Revolution explodes *its* local Chinese and Vietnamese families into the oblivion of an improving economy. Our generation has been transitional, instructed to follow economy, to look up to it like some admired uncle, and even most diligently, to send the next generation (our children) away to the better paying jobs of our imagination. The best paying jobs will always rob your sons and daughters of a future. College became a family wrecker after the existence of the North Atlantic Free Trade Agreement. And the Seneca Inn, for all it represents to me nostalgically, died the day Ray Kroc bewitched his first customer with a milkshake machine. I know and feel most unfortunately, that without the Seneca Inn, over half the population of my town and yours suffer some form of chronic psychosis.

Don't believe me? Just look at the arms of that waitress serving the cookies. She knows no joy but in the here today, here tomorrow.

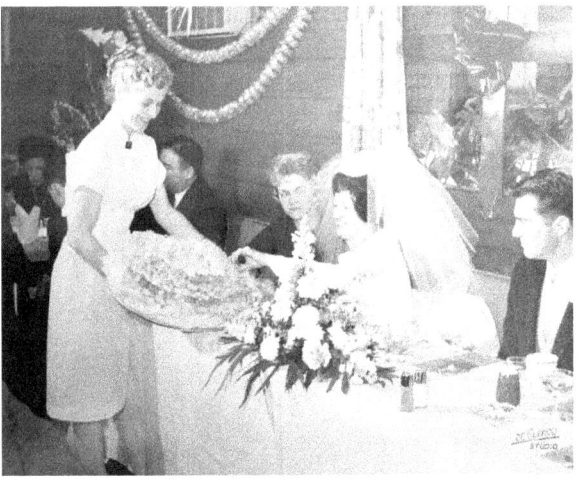

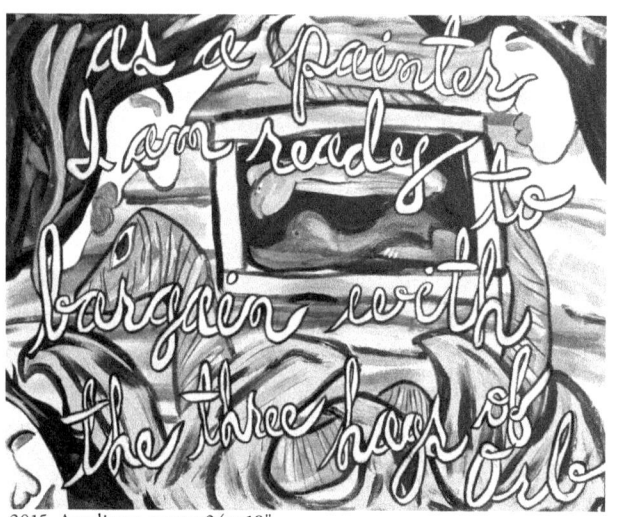

2015. Acrylic on canvas 24 x 18"

As a Painter I Am Ready to Bargain With the Three Hags of Orb

Art Dealers of America, please note that I am presently in negotiation with the bewitched forces that administer all art tolls of America. I am sitting in a hard chair in the center of a steel room surrounded by a gruesome, surly lot of well-dressed thousandaires. I will deal my life, my soul, a stack of hot pancakes for an invite into their paying society. A gavel just pounded and all humility flaked off my skin. Immediately I felt a whole lot better, if not as good, as the next guy. Several more rumbling grumbles, gesturing smiles from gleaming white partials, and a tall, thin woman in black suit asking if both the pancakes and my soul come with real maple syrup.

"Yes," I lie, and suddenly a thousand small birds of modesty shoot out my mouth encircling the room in sound and fury. Then silence and I stand up on the chair to wax poetic about the virtues of making maple syrup. "I tap the trees on Valentine's Day and wait for freezing nights followed by warm days. I collect the sap in five gallon buckets and begin boilng at the next ga-honk of V geese after the second robin sighting. I break branches over my knee, brave wind, rain and snow, stoke a crackling fire, watch the boil for hours and more, then pour the golden syrup in jars, and give it to you. I do it for nothing, and I am great. Now reach into your wallets and masturbate."

"Oohs and Ahhs" murmur throughout the room. Offers and deals. This one will pay for shipping and installation, but another says her outfit has a room in Soho where me and the wife can make pictures all day. Mr. G. has a private plane, but won't let me ride in it until someone is bribed to say I'm the best there is. The tall woman in black gets on her tip toes, calls out "Me!", and finally, I am represented by a gallery.

I am a working painter seeking representation in a big city gallery. There must be some market I can crawl into besides the snow blowing over snow one.

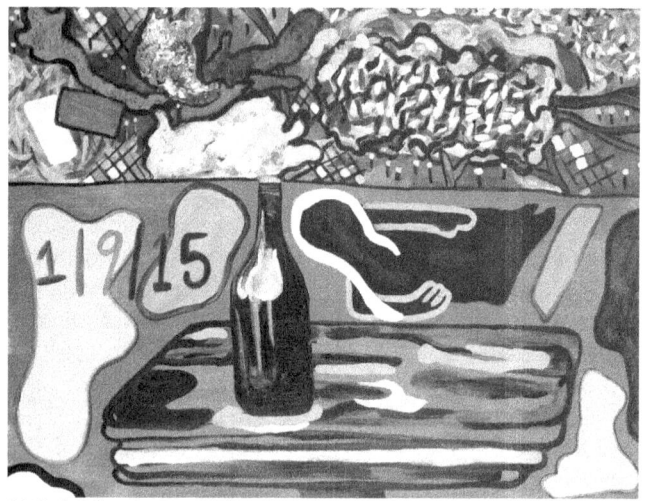

2015. Acrylic on canvas, 24 x 18"

Still Life

For the next couple months I will try to complete paintings by fighting the urge to finish them with text. I want to take medium-sized canvases (up to 24 inches), and color them from start to finish in a day's work—not so much for brevity as for skill enhancement. Eventually, I want to hold the brush as an extension of my hands, though I need to make my hands collaborate deftly with my confidence. Every brush stroke must matter without mattering. A kind of worker bee Zen Buddhism. I need this to happen. I cannot call myself a painter until I can paint like a successful plumber solders copper pipe. I must finish the job on time, and walk away whistling in the know that there won't be any leaks. Only then will the evening bread nourish and the hoppy beer intoxicate.

I am turning onto the road of success failure. Purply pink skies in the east.

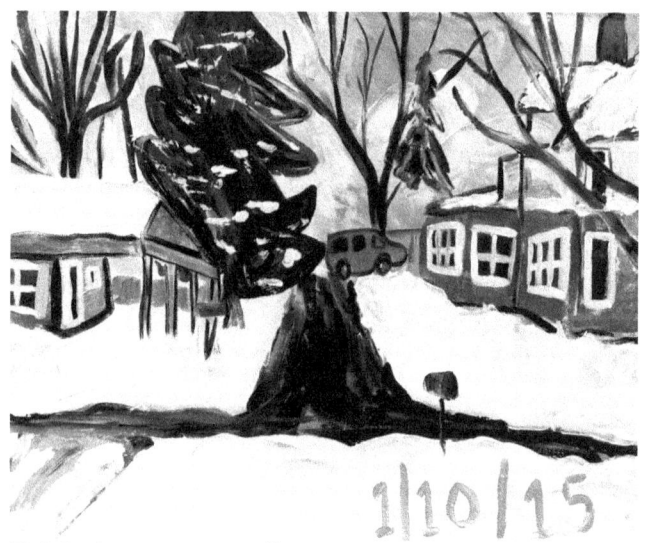

2015. Acrylic on canvas, 20 x 16"

Looking West Out the Window

The sun goes down so low in the south this time of year. Remember, no more text for a month or two—just 2 or 3 hour studies to teach my hand to speak with paint. In the mean time I will do laundry, make a stew, pet a cat. No one is watching. Nobody waits for what I do. Last night I watched a football game in my house for the second time in 14 years. I still don't know if I like to do this. After the game I got up off the couch and whizzed through several frantic chores to make up for being a painter with neither cafe nor commission. It felt easy like cheating. Then to a soft chair beneath a corner light to read my tome on Martin Luther King, Jr. Twenty-five years ago tomorrow I was reading from the same book the day my first daughter was born. Then I could watch football with less anxiety, paint a picture in a day, and still be a moving force in my daughter's life. I am frustrated with time. It is making me very anxious.

2015. Acrylic on canvas, 16 x 20"

Where I Make the Coldtonguecoldhamcoldbeefpickledgherkinssaladfrenchrollscresssandwidgespottedmeatgingerbeerlemonadesodawater

Sorry for the long title. It's what Ratty made in his tree trunk kitchen for picnicking on the lazy river with Mole from the 1908 smash hit novel, *Wind in the Willows*, by Kenneth Grahame. Row boating after quite a lot of work preparing and packing coldtonguecoldhamcoldbeefpickledgherkinssaladfrenchrollscresssandwidgespottedmeatgingerbeerlemonadesodawater.

This is a painting of my kitchen, where I spend the majority of my wakeful hours each day. Oops. I stuck a "J" in. Guess I couldn't resist the text. Still, a single letter besides "I" can't have an opinion that matters much anyway. My wife thought it referenced a jack-of-hearts in a card deck. No, it's the "J" in *Joy of Cooking*, by Rombauer and Rombauer Becker.

It's been twenty-odd years and I am still teaching myself to paint. These studies shall make a turning point in my vocation, which, because I rarely get paid, remains just a vacation.

Better get back to the chowder. There are those near and dear to me, who await my true worth as home-cook-who-paints.

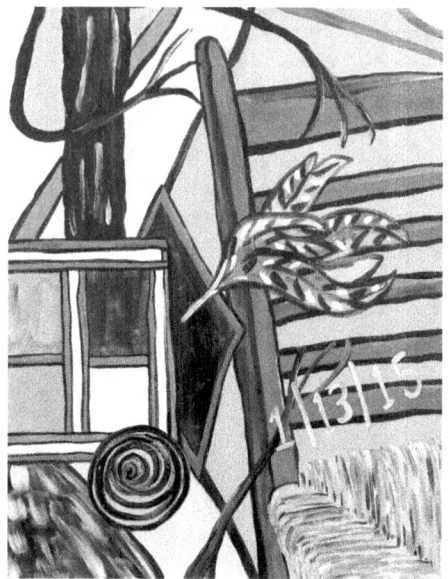

Chair 2015. Acrylic on canvas, 16 x 20"

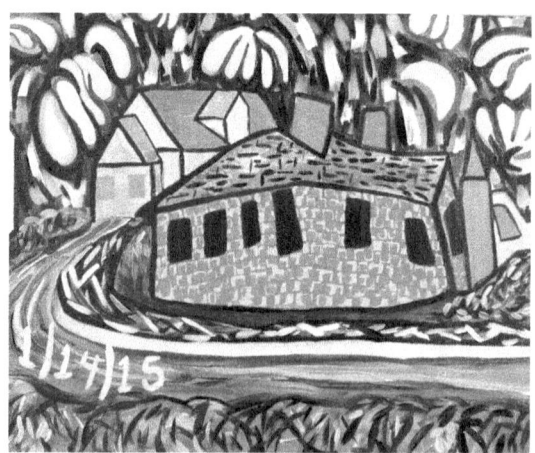

A Village My Canal Approves Of 2015. Acrylic on canvas, 20 x 16"

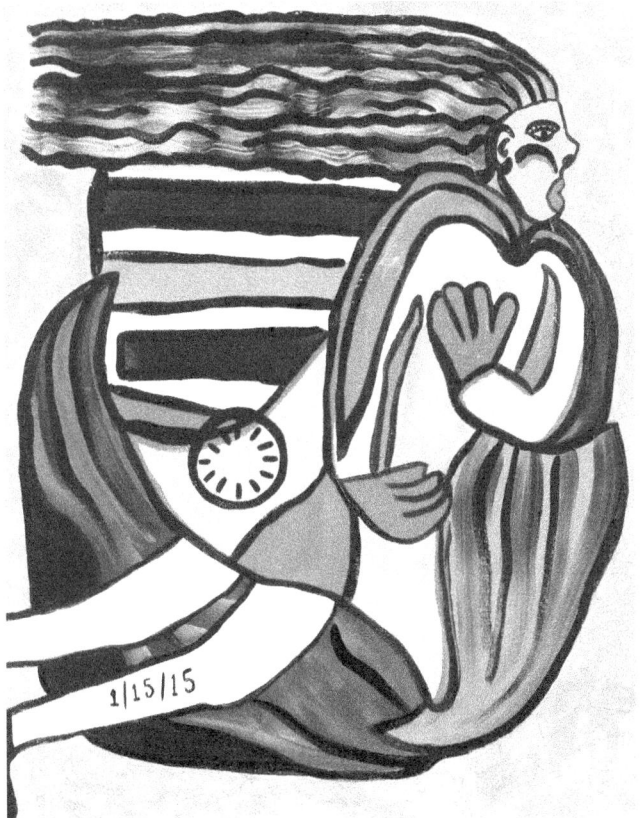

Past Aztec or Future Vermonter 2015. Acrylic on canvas, 16 x 20"

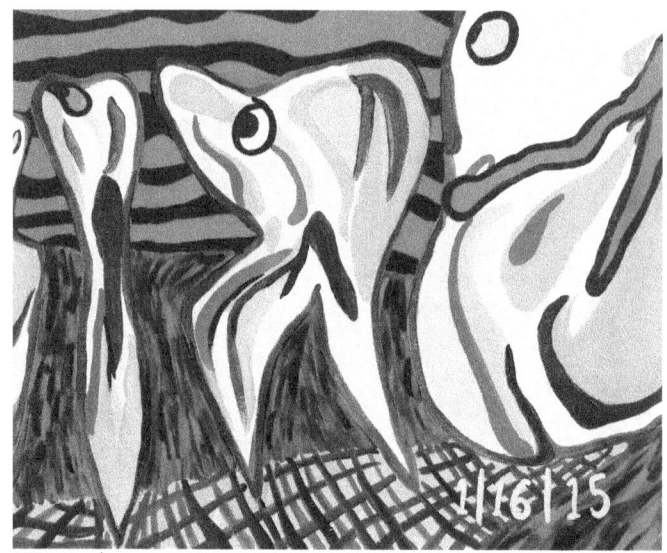

2015. Acrylic on canvas, 20 x 16"

My Teeth Overhear Their Fate From the Periodontist

I guess teeth have ears. They should have brains enough to know
I can't afford to lose them. Don't worry. boys. I will go for the deep
cleaning, gargle with salt water 3X daily, and apply a paste of garlic
and milk along my gum line. Yes I admit, I made a painting to
remember you by, just in case my ship comes in.

Now, about that ship...

I am looking for advice from other producers of original mate-
rial. How do you convert your works to currency? I am in earnest.
The Internet has not helped, neither has peddling colored canvases
and books in my neighborhood. I have had many solo shows, lawn
sales, Internet posts. Nothing. Nada times nothing. For instance,
last year I published a book that even my—wait... Not true. My
mother *did* buy it. But she was the only one.

It's not like I overprice my work. $14 for a book is not exorbitant.
Last night I paid that much for red curry. And it's already gone.
Geeze, I didn't even like it enough to keep it. Couldn't tell you if
there was basil in it or not. And it's not like I had to have the curry
because it's food, and need it to stay alive. A foraged apple would
have sufficed. Or I could have refrained from dinner, saved gain-
ing a half pound, and awoke this morning able to button my jeans.

I have theories about this starving artist dilemma. Many spring
from the field of social psychology. Here is one:

None of us are any good until many of us say that some of us are.

Each failed writer or painter needs, more than talent, a promoter
with Biblical outreach. If Beyoncé (accent on the e) wore the teeth
image to don her Super Bowl outfit, I would be rich and known
richly by morning. Target would call for a wall hanging product
line, and the New York Times would best seller me. If Oprah got
caught reading less trite and inane crap, maybe some of you talented writers could afford rent as well as dinner, and miraculously the
Media-CIA Industrial Complex would suffer sinking ratings of its
perpetually popular "Let's Dumb Down America".

All fine literature, music, and art is relegated to obscurity if not
considered salable by a connected media entity. Here is a rejection
from a book publisher I received a couple weeks ago, followed
by a quote from Henry Miller who wrote meaningful desk chair

philosophy at a time when art was the artist, and not bullhorn announcements from high-rise promoters about the "state of the art money".

You do seem passionate and, as you wrote, "determined," so I'm sure this won't stop you at all from continuing your search for a publisher. I would like to suggest you consider self-publishing this manuscript. Just from reading the first sample parts you sent me I can tell you it's going to be a very difficult sell to any indie press. Forget about even going to the majors via a literary agent. **It occupies too much head space, in my opinion**, *and while that's not a bad thing at all for some readers who enjoy that sort of thing, commercially this would be extremely difficult to convince anyone to spend any money on reading your words. Even if you have some clout due to your painting,* **it is pretty thick stuff to get into and stay into**. *I don't mean this to sound mean at all. I just feel that this is the kind of book that may have a life as a self-published work. Save yourself the time and trouble of querying anyone else and publish it yourself, then I would suggest perhaps focus more on the marketing end of the book rather than getting one of us snobby publishers to approve it lol. I hope you'll agree.*

A nice, honest rejection. I agree with him. I prefer to self-publish. But to make me a marketer of my own work is like asking a corn farmer to peddle boil-in-a-bag on the street corner. Doomed to failure before the manure is spread.

My reply:

Thank you for a fast response and helpful criticism. Self publishing is the right way to go. Whitman peddled "Leaves of Grass" door-to-door, and look where that got him! No one then (or today) would publish Whitman's work to make a living. For me, it has become some personal badge of honor to be an unread writer. Like threshing wheat over a storm water grate. Very nothing, and yet some thing very good too.

Just doesn't pay the bills.

Here is Henry Miller:

Most of the young men of talent whom I have met in this country give one the impression of being somewhat demented. Why shouldn't they? They are living amidst spiritual gorillas, living with food and drink maniacs, success mongers, gadget innovators, pub-

licity hounds. God, if I were a young man today, if I were faced with
a world such as we have created, I would blow my brains out. Or,
perhaps like Socrates, I would walk into the market place and spill
my seed on the ground. I would certainly never think to write a book
or paint a picture or compose a piece of music. For whom? Who
beside a handful of desperate souls can recognize a work of art?
What can you do with yourself if your life is dedicated to beauty?
Do you want to face the prospect of spending the rest of your life in a
straight-jacket?

I suggest all writers to read Miller, as Miller wanted to be read.
Read me first. He'd dead. And I could use an art-paid-for loaf of
bread.

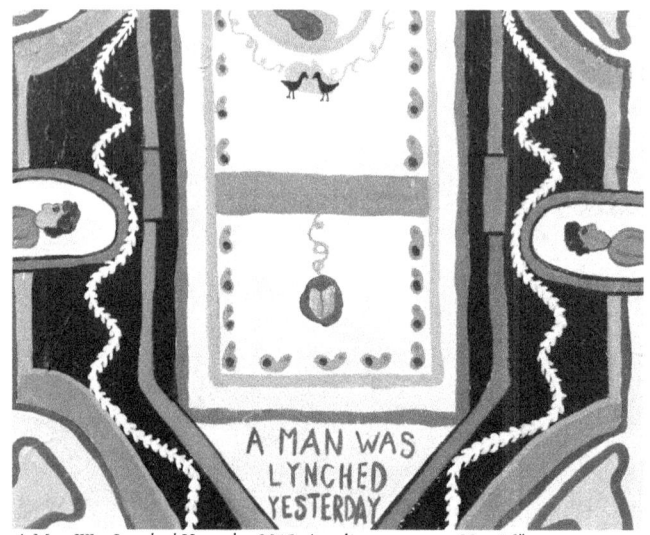

A Man Was Lynched Yesterday 2015. Acrylic on canvas, 20 x 16"

Washington D.C. Maker's Mark Musings

In February, my sculptor friend Eric and I took a road trip to the mouth of the Patuxent River in Maryland. He got his work accepted into a national show and I offered to be his assistant for delivery and set up. Great time. Glad he had me along. We stopped in D.C. to take in the sites for the day. Eric went his way and I went mine. From the Library of Congress® I walked the National Mall, took a right at the Lincoln Memorial, and crossed several alphabet streets before taking a left at M Street into Georgetown. I went into an old man bar on Wisconsin Avenue and ordered a double Maker's Mark® on ice while the veins in my feet pulsated pain. The bartender gave me a heavy pour and I slipped into a highly relaxed, booze-induced, confident state of mind recounting the thoughts I had along my Capital walk. I had it all figured out. The facade broke. The wizard in the hall. Don't pay any attention to the man behind the curtain! At first blush, it all seemed so attainable. The Smithsonian with its startling array of art and artifact, and every house of government open and inviting to all and sundry. Beyond the entryways, and the four or five security guards running the metal detectors, palatial grandeur graciously shared among all who would bother to come. Once the sites were taken in, however, the old Ron sensory cynicism crept up the brain stem to assess. Or was it the 90 proof bourbon?

A closer look would discover the smoke and mirrors.

I should have just finished the drink, met up with my friend for dinner, and got out of town joyful after an inspirational tour of our national city. Instead, I talked to myself in the head, remembering the high volume of dandys dressed in three-quarter length black coats, dark scarves, black shoes, and impeccably manicured heads, walking to and from what had to be the most important meetings ever scheduled on planet earth. I linked their public personas to possessing one of three highly paid professions: lawyer, lobbyist, or lackey, busy working their avarice for private gain. To me, each could not have appeared more silly, more pathetic, and as a class, amounting to no higher state of nirvana than eager gophers to "Hey Spiking" the old men of the White League (aka: the three branches of government). Silly and yet incredibly dangerous.

Their comings and goings were what tipped me off, always on another side of the road, looking straight ahead, paying no attention
to the rubber necking all around them. Ah-ha! My friend and I
were not welcome. Beyond day-tripping, this was never to be our
city. The planes flying overhead, the military chopper circling the
Smithsonian, the hundreds of police and guards on patrol were
there to bolster the facade and promote the grand illusion; that is,
to make the Americans visiting the Capital believe they are a special people, that this land is their land, and the politicians elected
to work in these ornate palaces are here working for the overall
good of the nation. I have always thought this a fantasy, held up
by a shoestring of economic good fortune. Just outside the federal
government compound, in D.C. proper, there were 105 homicides
last year. I brought up a graphic to see where all the violence was
happening. The exact path I took to Georgetown was untouched
by violent death the whole year. That means, the lives in the government district were protected, and all the people on the outside
left to fend for themselves. Sounds like any good dystopian novel
plot. Mountains of national money used to protect the sycophants
and their masters, and to Hell with Americans you, me, and the
rest of D.C.

So when the President* talks to us "folks" on any Super Bowl
Sunday, I now know (as I once suspected), that he is addressing
Mr. and Mrs. Peon, or Ron the painter, or the average Joe family
on holiday in D.C. He's telling us in plain doublespeak to have a
nice time visiting his city, and then get the Hell out, back to the
routine monotony that fuels the power we will never understand,
at least by the machinations of what is provided to us gratis on a
sight-seeing trip to America's free capital city.

Anyway, I had a good time with Eric for the rest of the evening. The booze wore off. We dined fork-free on Ethiopian cuisine.
And I paid no more attention to the made up stories that I cannot
translate into sense, no matter how hard I try. The library had a
nice exhibition on Civil Rights though, as if it were a special time
of the past. Over now, and let's carry on with the greatness of our
nation. Just pay no attention to the man behind the curtain! Next
door there was a Supreme Court*. It too probably thinks without
irony that it helped people of color achieve their ends. Dred Scott
sat beneath the thirty foot ceiling waiting for great wise men to

tell him that he was property after all. Even after the invention and wide-scale use of the railroad! And a hundred years later mobs lynched men, but only because they could get away with it. 105 murders in Washington D.C. last year. All that money and machinery, and who does it really protect?

No one of any account.

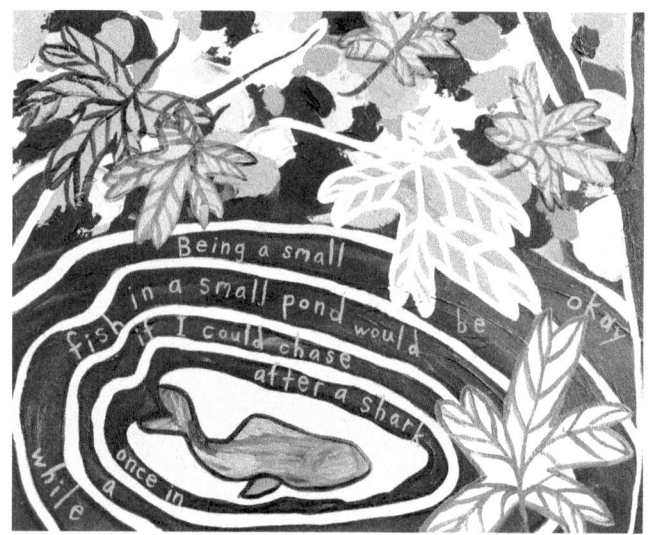

Being a small fish in a small pond would be okay if I could chase after a shark once in a while a

2015. Acrylic on canvas, 20 x 16"

Being a Small Fish in a Small Pond Would Be Okay If I Could Chase After a Shark Once In a While

I think I shall take the gloves off now and wrap my hands in writhing snakes. I cannot get a gallery to interview me with port-folio, let alone write back a rejection of any kind. My wife says we should dig a tunnel through the snow out to the street and set a "painting of the day" between two luminaries. A sign reads, "Drop a coin into the box if you'd like to see another tomorrow". Maybe the mailman will toss in a dime. Who knows?

This painting illustrates what the director of Any Gallery in New York City can think about after reading my query. "He is a nobody. He hasn't $2000.00/month for a studio with smudged windows and lingering smells of rat pee. Small fish, small pond."

Oh well, I paint in the cellar. I paint in the kitchen. I dream about taking a car to a southern beach and painting pelicans. I understand I do not make beauty; there are millions upon millions of more glorious talents respiring today. But I do make. I do create. At times the great spirit is seated inside me nodding of success that has already come. The children are wise in a weary world. The wife still keeps a little wonder left for me. And my fortunate good health frees my mind to feeling like the eager child on a new morning.

Other times I am a realist of the human world, a fool and a failure, who thinks he needs some phony wannabe in the big city to authenticate his genius. Even at this low I realize it can never work. Our lives could not be more unknown to each other if he was a calamari and I a Gila monster. The human world is fraught with unhappy competition. On bad days it woos me. On good days I paint and care for a family.

Thinking out loud can be messy. But at least I am still thinking.

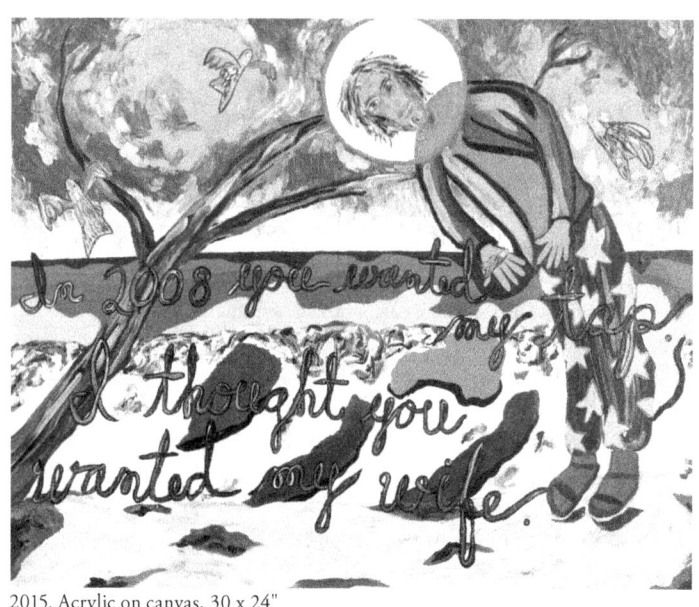

2015. Acrylic on canvas, 30 x 24"

In 2008 You Wanted My Tap. I Thought You Wanted My Wife

My friend Dan is finishing his last winter here in the exhaust-smear-on-snow state. I met him at a local art show in 2008. I was living in the country then. He came up to me, hand outstretched, in all his Texas friendly to say hello. I pulled my hand out of my winter coat and there was a maple tap in it. He asked me what the heck it was, and then after I told him, he did that big Texas thing that scares us tight New Yorkers to new heights of paranoia; he asked if he could come over to my place and watch me maple syrup. My wife was there. He kept looking at me, then her, waiting for an answer. It was the first time a stranger ever asked me to do anything, let alone invite himself over to my house to play. Oh, no doubt he just wanted to get closer to my wife, kill me later, and then marry her.

This painting is one of several I will complete for his going away party. They will be auctioned off to raise money for one of the most enthusiastic people ever to step foot into my bland habitat.

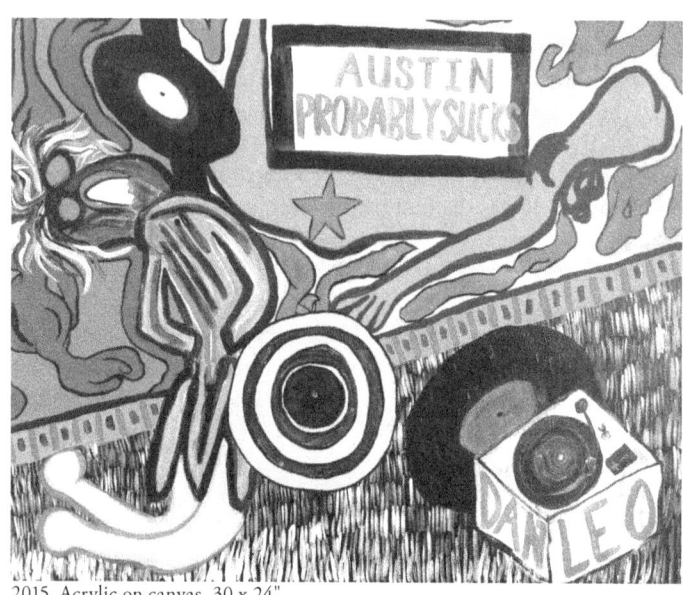

2015. Acrylic on canvas, 30 x 24"

Austin Probably Sucks

Who knows? Probably not even Austinians. I just want to pummel the notion of better places. I don't believe they exist. My friend is leaving the cold, miserable economy of Lake Ontario. I can't blame him. It was all downhill after the automobile came into fashion. Still, we hold on dearly to our illusions, and dream of better places right up to the last cough. Some say meditation might take us to "here is the best place to be". I guess I could tap into that magic next winter beside my Happy Lite®. I'm gonna miss Dan, even if Austin probably sucks.

In the painting his alter-ego ghost dances with his lone star illusions. I now dance the emptiness I'll feel a few months after he leaves this dead horse town.

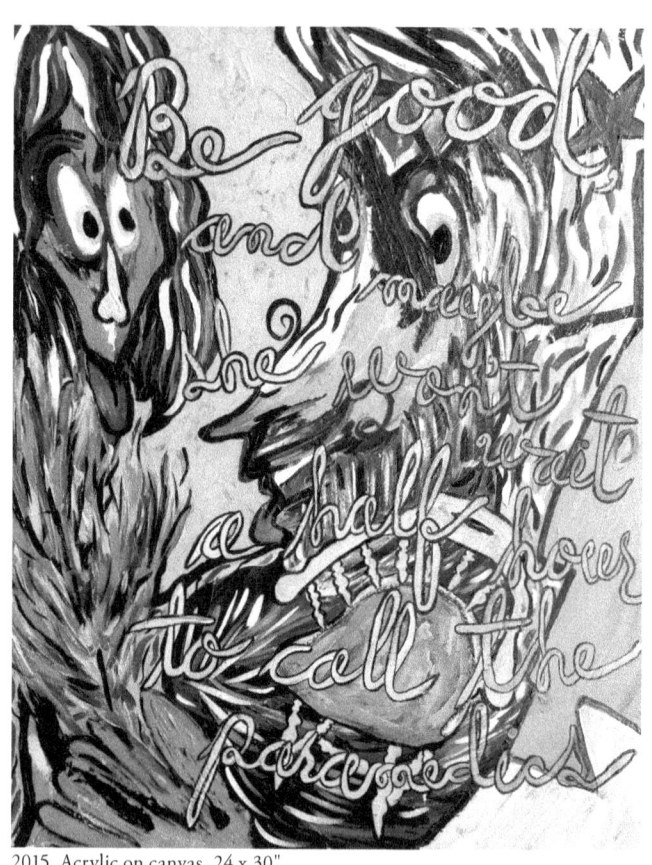

2015. Acrylic on canvas, 24 x 30"

Be Good and Maybe She Won't Wait a Half Hour to Call the Paramedics

Here is one of many I will paint for my friend Dan's going away party in June. It's what I can do. I hope that many show up to the extravaganza to purchase them at high bids—all the money will go to him with the promise to feed my family if ever we visit Texas.

Dan is a giver and receiver. However, in this life, he has given more of himself than anyone I have heard about—including Buddha and St. Francis.

This painting is the story of Dan's step grandfather and his heart attack chair. Dan brought it to me last year. It has saved my back in the studio, and I have painted more dutifully because of it. Anyway, Dan told me his grandmother was abused by the chair's owner for many years of her life. The day his step grandfather had a heart attack, and fell off the chair onto the floor, she waited a half hour to call the paramedics. They pronounced him dead at the scene. Granddad could have carried over to the next world with cherished love and pride if he just refrained from locking grandma up in a room whenever the urge overtook him.

Boys will be boys, and sometimes privately express themselves as squealing piglets terrified of the day-to-day world. Some do this while painting from an old chair. Others get off the chair from time to time to beat their wives down to the floor.

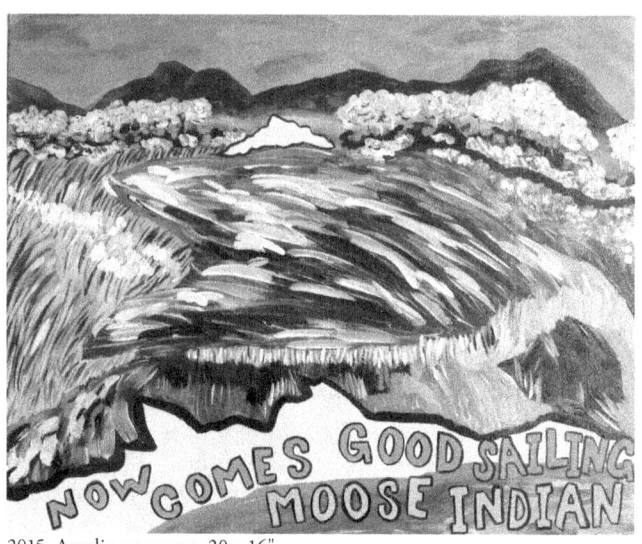

2015. Acrylic on canvas, 20 x 16"

Now Comes Good Sailing Moose Indian

These are Henry Thoreau's last words. Think long pauses between tuberculosis breaths. He is a distant relative of mine, not like a distant that we all share with someone like "Lucy" the Rift Valley Girl. Actually, I am blood related to the great philosopher. A strand of his DNA would be nice to test for what I hypothesize to be the cuckoo gene that traveled six generations and infinite possibilities to my father's 23 surprises gifted on consummation day.

Come to think of it, I might have more of him than less. I have an inordinate amount of will power, a love of the natural world, aloneness tendencies, and, I am a horrible dresser. What I didn't get (his way with words) is oh so obvious. So in the morning I paint what I can on canvas and then go sound a lake for an afternoon. "Better to be a living dog than a dead lion," eh cousin?

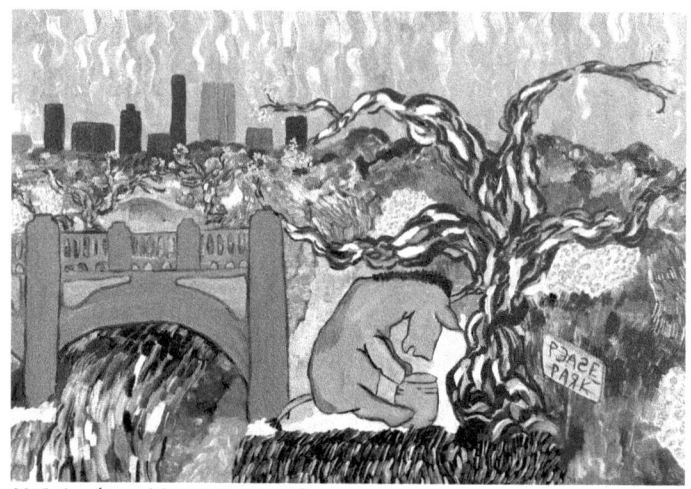

2015. Acrylic on Masonite®, 20 x 13"

Eeyore Finds His Honey at Pease Park

Every two years The New York Foundation of the Arts offers a $7,000.00 grant to artists of several disciplines, of which painting is one. I have been applying since 2008. It is very competitive and tends to award where the competition is clustered—the five boroughs of NYC. I don't think anyone from my county has ever been granted this generous prize.

I no longer protect delusions of hope in this state of the art. Here is the cover letter anyway. The judges aren't supposed to read it before judging (but I know they do):

"These are recent works painted within the last year. I paint every day but Sunday. My wife supports my financial needs. I am also a writer, and like Kenneth Patchen, will sneak text into my work, even if it only repeats the title. Unlike Kenneth, and more like Picasso I would prefer to be a rich man so that I could live like a pauper. These paintings have energy. They are vibrant and moving. I don't wish to be clever. I need to communicate. I live next door to a college in a poor county. I have house shows to expose my work. I invite faculty. Yet even the art professors make a wide berth on opening night. I am not tired of rejection. I just expect it. Like the Beat poets of 1950's San Francisco, these paintings need to be read aloud with jugs of wine passed around. So please, get up from your chairs and have a drink.

Emerson wrote that the future novels will tend more towards autobiography, one person talking to another about the concerns of his own heart. Painters are their own culture, never one drawn along national, racial or ethnic lines. The great art houses, promoters, gallerists, and art historians have warped the joy of painting into categories of success or failure both determined by finance. We forget that van Gogh was destitute all his professional life. We know the story of he and Gauguin in Arles. Men. Dreamers. But above all, painters in determination. There are no more movements as long as we allow this pandering to the unartists, Koons and Hirst. Just clever-Eddies with their billionaire Dubai cohorts. A great American art collector today owns a football team. Enough said about culture. His life alone makes certain that the art market turns the humble painter into an impractical beggar.

Impressionists roll in their graves. They used to meet in cafes to discuss their work, but also subjects on politics, rage and love. Culture for the first modern painters was to be among others of like mind. Not so much today. After a brief jag mixing and applying color to canvas, the hyper-individual artist visits the cafe to pick up a latte to go. Reality TV tonight. Netflix has a new series. Maybe he'll get inspired in the morning with a great idea for another gnostic artist statement to present alone, in an e-mail, from his computer, in a room, with nobody. Some culture! I dream a future for the painter that connects him to others of like mind. Not on Facebook either. Not that dystopian billionaire's cash cow! No, we must meet in the cafe to give the college grads of tomorrow an essay on art that doesn't read like a crafty tome of a tax write off.

I am just so tired of the make-believe network! Damn you! Look at my work with me standing beside it. Tell me what you think. Tell me what you think!"

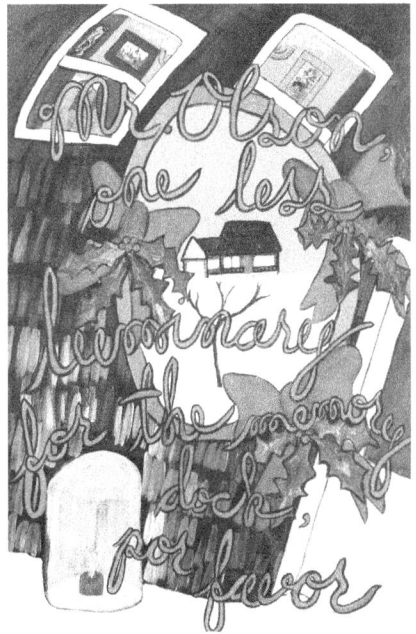

2015. Acrylic on Masonite®, 13 x 20"

Mr. Olson, One Less Luminary For the Memory Dock, Por Favor

Another painting for Dan's escape from New York. The great American sculptor, Mr. Olson, performs a hit-and-run ice luminary to several doors at Christmastime. Always much better than a flaming paper bag, one opens the door to discover a candle lit in a giant frozen sconce. Luminary can be an artificial light or a person who inspires and influences others. At 43.5° latitude, our winter town cannot afford to lose one of the last aristocrats of the spirit. We lost another a couple year's back, but she shared a luminary with the high boss of culture. This will be the first and only painting depicting my loss. I want to celebrate Dan's departure. Maybe Texas will welcome him home as much as New York shunned his enthusiasm.

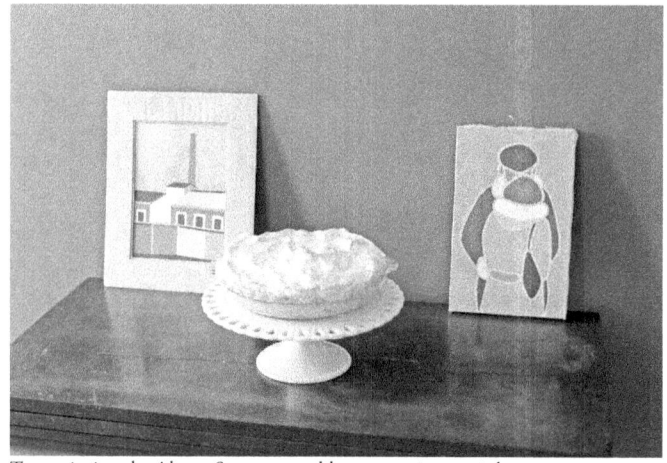

Two paintings by Alexey Stepanov and lemon meringue pie by me.

When a Stuckist Trades, Does a Tree Fall in the Woods?

Last month, via Facebook, I contacted a painter living in Moscow to ask if he would sell me one of his paintings. His name is Alexey Stepanov and I find his work to be pure genius. I like it mostly, I guess, because it is good, and isn't mine. I wanted to save the money up by September for an October birthday present to give to my wife. This was a big step for me. I usually keep to my own self in matters of discomfiting. I expected a big Russian, "Ha! You want me to sell my work on American layaway? Go jump in the Moskva!"

Instead, he suggested we trade. I don't know Russian. His English is bad, and the Internet translator he connects to, translates my messages into nonsense—for example—"I painting like a dog eat with my wife a moon the size pickling".

He agreed to send me the painting I desired, Lovers, an 8 x 10 inch, to keep shipping costs low. And I picked out a small triptych for him. When he found out I was sending three, he threw another one of his into the bargain. The Red Pipe, a landscape that reminds me of the town I live in.

Magic feeling. I am still on a high. His suggesting this trade, the follow through, the kindness, the reverence, means more to my soul than if some billion-millionaire sent Triscuit® suits to my door to buy up the entire basement archive.

A painter admiring the work of another painter. Fuel to continue.

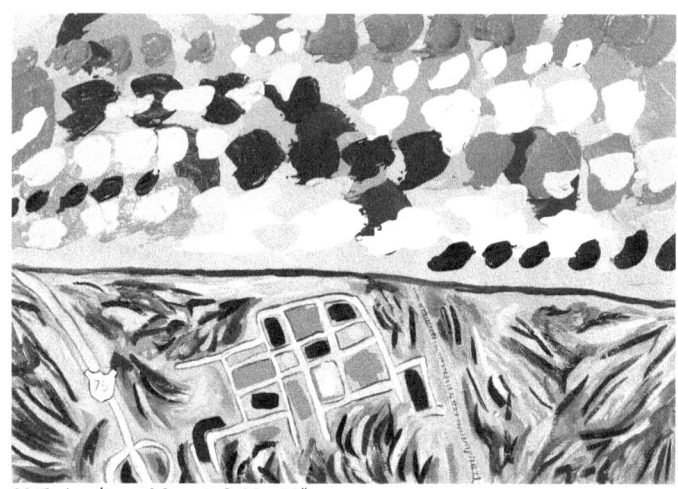

2015. Acrylic on Masonite®, 20 x 13"

Methodical Storm Clouds Form Over Anna, Texas. Ralph Fults Takes To Highway Robbery

My friend Dan is counting his change to save up for his return to Texas. He took my moldy bottles left on the side of the road for the garbage men. I was too rich to spend the twenty minutes washing them to raise 65 cents. Or, as Dan reminded me, 78 cents to the 6 cent bottle return on the other side of town. So with my extra time, I begin a painting with a higher end in mind. Dan is an expert for making small monies work for big courage. But I am a philosopher. If I cannot get bottle return bids in exchange for the personality expressed in these paintings, then Dan will go to hell in Texas, or any outpost of dystopia where humans feel they need to sell precious time for chump change.

Dan needs money. But if I cannot raise it for him with paint, then he must come to terms with his own neurosis. If wealth was the chief end for all, earth would have exploded long, long ago.

These paintings and many more will go on auction at 7:00 a.m. on June 5, 2015, and will stay online (ebay) for seven days. A reserve bid of 78 cents for each won't stop humanity from trying to exchange their bottles and eat the painter too. It may be a fact that, unlike a used beer bottle, no modern house will bid on a Throop painting to hang. It's not full of fluffy mold, nor rimmed with some user's lip smear to wash away.

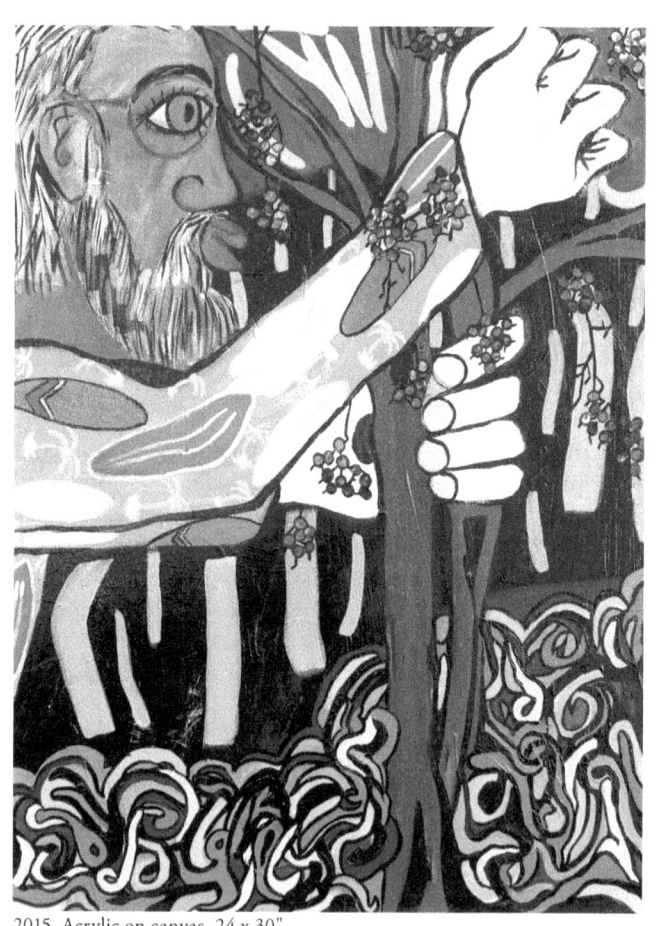

2015. Acrylic on canvas, 24 x 30"

Dan Picking Elderberries On Hot August Night

Yesterday I asked Dan if Texas gets dandelions in the springtime. It does, yet he will miss the yellow petal harvest this year. His first rest stop in the giant state lies about fifty miles northeast of Dallas. He wants to work his way down to Austin eventually. Any readers have jobs available in either area? Dan is 58 years old holding a B.F.A. degree from University of Texas. He is a good, honest father and friend. His skills are people, teaching and foraging. His hobbies—art, wine and beer making. For an interview, watch a football game with him. He comes to your house with fixins' for burritos, a bag of chotskies to hand out, and year old NY Times Arts sections. He pours you a tall craft beer with the enthusiasm of a cloistered monk. Hiring him will improve your life tremendously. He doesn't steal. He barters. And makes you feel like you could always do a little bit more to be good.

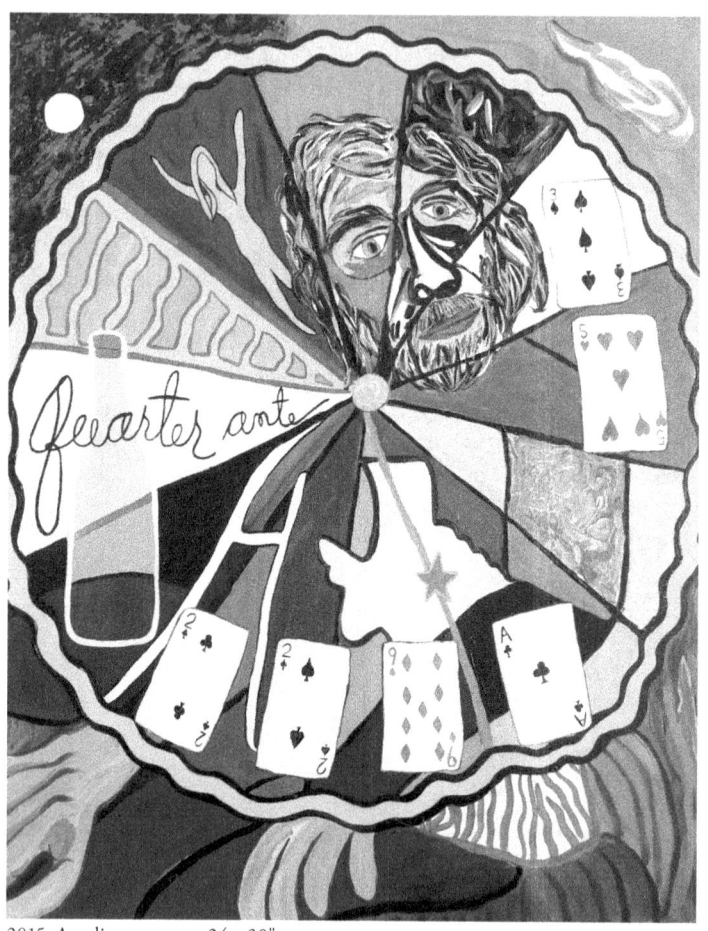

2015. Acrylic on canvas, 24 x 30"

Dan Plays Texas Hold 'Em With Bad Hand

Another piece to auction at Dan's going-away party. I have too many paintings for the friends we keep.

This morning I will clean out the refrigerator and pick dandelions for wine. But for now, a quote from Emerson that has cured me of temporary creative paralysis time and again.

Life is a succession of lessons which must be lived to be understood. All is riddle, and the key to a riddle is another riddle. There are as many pillows of illusion as flakes in a snowstorm. We wake from one dream into another dream. The toys, to be sure, are various, and are graduated in refinement to the quality of the dupe. The intellectual man requires a fine bait; the sots are easily amused. But everybody is drugged with his own frenzy, and the pageant marches at all hours, with music and banner and badge.

However, Thoreau, friend and land squatter to Ralph Waldo, was the truer philosopher.

If the day and the night are such that you greet them with joy, and life emits a fragrance like flowers and sweet-scented herbs, is more elastic, more starry, more immortal—that is your success. All nature is your congratulation, and you have cause momentarily to bless yourself. The greatest gains and values are farthest from being appreciated. We easily come to doubt if they exist. We soon forget them. They are the highest reality. Perhaps the facts most astounding and most real are never communicated by man to man. The true harvest of my daily life is somewhat as intangible and indescribable as the tints of morning or evening. It is a little star-dust caught, a segment of the rainbow which I have clutched.

Delivering Thoreau's eulogy, Emerson made a jab at his late friend, telling the audience that Henry was more prone to sow beans than success, implying that Thoreau wasted his talents on nothing much really. As a younger man, I stopped reading Emerson after I came upon his funeral insult. He was only a man of his time, an intellectual Lady Gaga, seeking applause and money, not satori. Just making a name for himself, so he could die with a name. Emerson was drugged with his own frenzy, but Thoreau was high on an unpopular life.

My kind of philosopher.

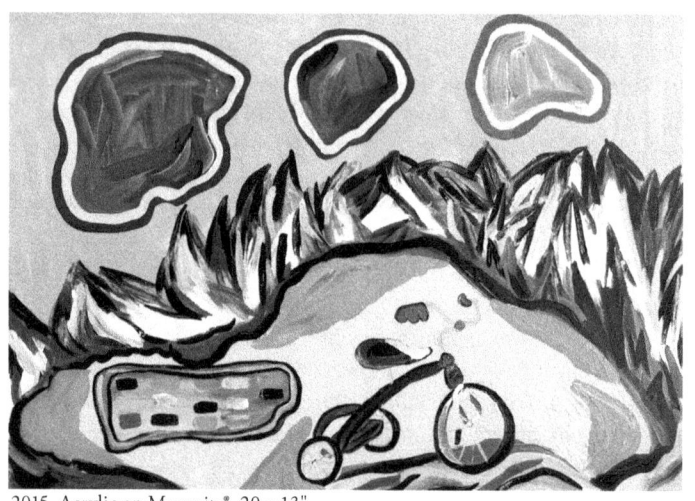

2015. Acrylic on Masonite®, 20 x 13"

Dan, Beware Waco, Where the Biker Gangs Might Make You Play Candy Crush on a Smartphone

Dan is off to Texas in a month. With this painting I want to warn him of the dangers of people texting and phone stroking at the same time while riding a bike.

Last month's biker bar shootout was bad news. I saw photos coming over the wire. Bikers were rounded up and made to sit down along the curbs of the mall parking lot. One photo showed an arrested man with a trimmed beard looking at his smartphone. A hipster Harley dude packing iPhone heat, who might inspire fear sparks in any small town or city if he didn't look so darn silly with that phone. And you just know he has a bells and whistles Harley payment on top of his Verizon contract. Probably pays his mortgage and utilities on time and frets over extra money for fuel and food.

Groupthink feeds on the stuff of Harleys and holocausts. Once, maybe a century and a half ago, America was a land of individuals. If an economy had room, a man could live a whole life without the adult urge to sew Chinese printed bald eagle decals onto a jean jacket made in Paraguay. Even further back, a Boston Massacre was a good story for an upcoming national revolution. Five people were killed for throwing snowballs. Today, 200 narcissists with trimmed beards cannot refrain from acting out their "me, me, me!" fantasies in a rumble at the mall without killing each other. We are a nation far removed from our own recent past. These poor chumpy fellows have been raised without any idea as to what an individual is. Now they are arrested for life because each one made a snap judgment to follow the lead of the degenerate standing beside him. An excellent case study for sociologists. There could be room for empathy from locals in the town and county who see and, most unfortunately, *hear* them ride by in their silly-willy gang uniforms, but they're an ignorant, dangerous band of rowdies, and a barrier for my friend Dan, the individual man, who meets his life and does not call it names. I don't like groups. They make biker gangs and Pentagons. Even those that swear they live by the forces of good, say a church committee, raising money to "save" a village in Guatemala. Good or bad, too much time is spent pining for initiation into and maintaining the group, rather than apply-ing my grandmother's long time common sense proverb, "charity begins at home," to every day encounters with adversity. Suddenly, after years of raising Billy to be a good Christian, he's out shooting sticks or stones at any one who calls him names. Or any one whom his boss said called him a name. Or any one who has not been "named" in the group he belongs to.

Just be super careful in Texas Dan. I hear everything there is big. Especially the big fiefdoms of the silly-dangerous babies out riding on their minibikes.

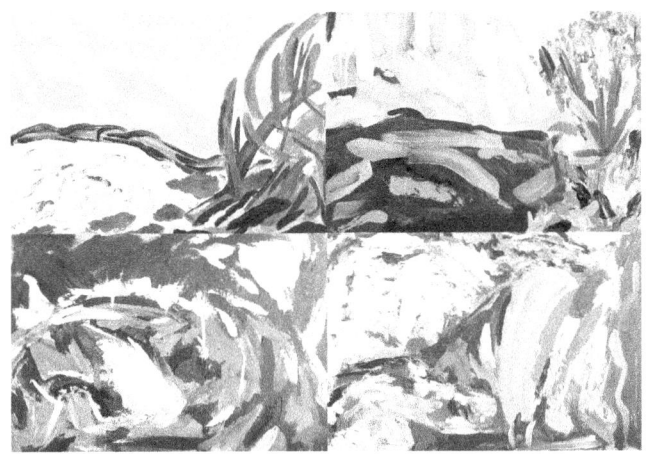

2015. Acrylic on Masonite®, (4) 20 x 13"

Winter, Spring, Summer, Fall, You Can Call, But I Probably Won't Let You Stay Fearing You'll Take Over the House

Same lake, different look through the seasons. I went easy on winter (top left), which is normally a frozen dead white shorescape with an occasional cold steel or polar blue sky. I'll frame it this morning in disassembled futon pine Dan gave me last night while he cleaned out his storage shed for the yard sale. He has over thirty years of accumulated savings to hawk. This includes among count-less treasures, a rusty tin man oil can, an official Pee Wee Herman pull-the-string doll, *A Perry Cuomo Christmas* on 78, art books to the ceiling, mason jars, wine bottles, wood snowshoes, tie-dyed tapestries, and a Ted Williams 7 hp boat motor.

Dan will be a free man. He'll leave for Texas in a van. I will con-tinue to paint his pre-odyssey departure because, as a light fool, I believe it will actually bring a traveling fortune to Dan. Heck, if he can carry a Pee Wee Herman doll on his back for thirty years, I can hobby as a delusional painter-fundraiser. Around here village idiots are easily ignored as long as their spouses can keep up with a car payment.

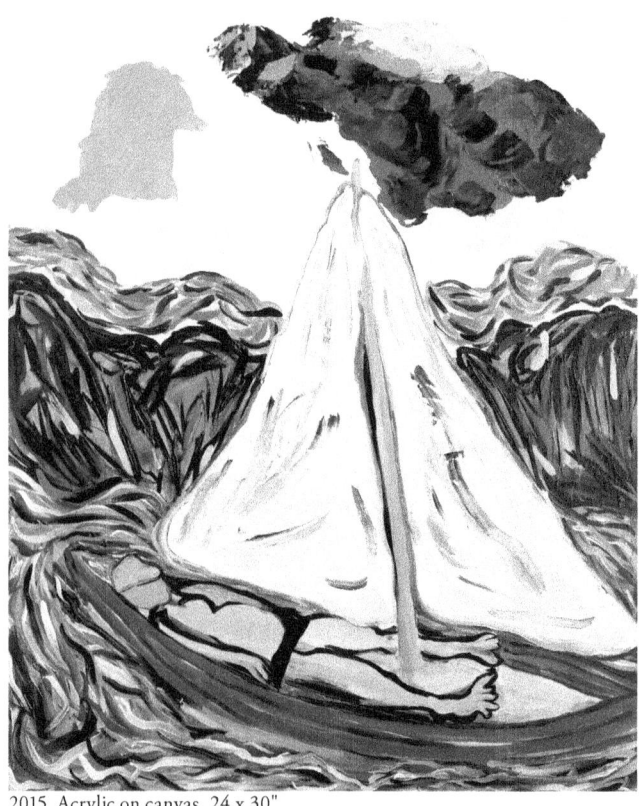

2015. Acrylic on canvas, 24 x 30"

Dan Sails Lake Travahalla

Still applying paint to mostly two-dimensional surface to stimulate money-giving at my friend Dan's going-away party. If any one is interested, I can offer a reserve bid discount of one gallon of mid-Atlantic state gasoline. Most likely Pennsylvania. The van will be stuffed out the windows with just a tiny fraction of Dan's stuff accumulations to weigh down mileage significantly. Each painting at the party will have a similar reserve bid. The cost of a fast food stop, an overnight stay at a state park, a souvenir for his boy, etc.

Here is Dan in an ambiguous posture floating on Lake Travis outside Austin, Texas. Is he a viking being sent off to paradise, or a prodigal Texan seeking minimum wage work?

For those living in Texas, and who have picked the latter, please consider hiring Dan. He has a Bachelor of Fine Arts degree, over twelve years experience teaching, and a voracious enthusiasm that is magnified to wild enthusiasm whenever money is a potential outcome in a venture. He is personable, sober, thoughtful, empathetic,and presently unemployed. I offer the pick of up to ten paintings for the reader who can offer Dan a steady job in the greater Dallas or Austin metropolitan area.

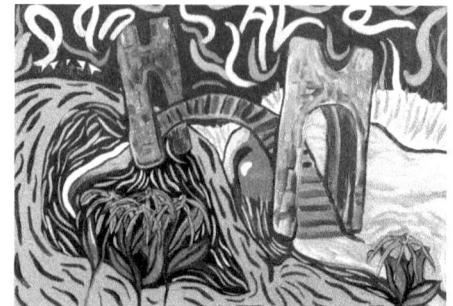

Dan Made Existentialism Fun 2015. Acrylic on Masonite®, 20 x 13"

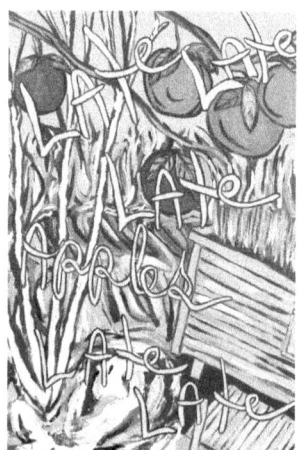

Late Late Late Apples 2015. Acrylic on Masonite®, 13 x 20"

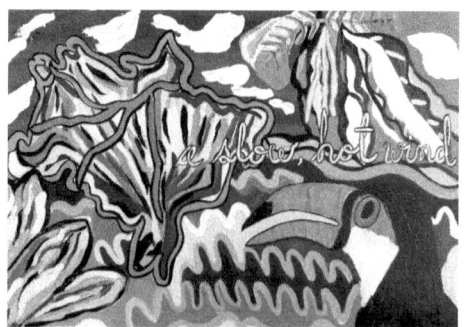

A Slow Hot Wind 2015. Acrylic on Masonite®, 20 x 13"

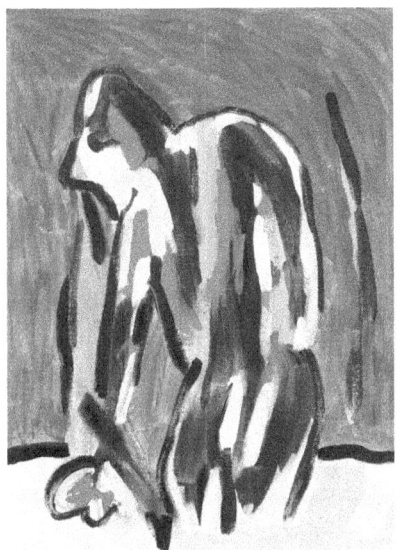

How Dan Thought After Catholicism 2015.
Acrylic on canvas, 16 x 20"

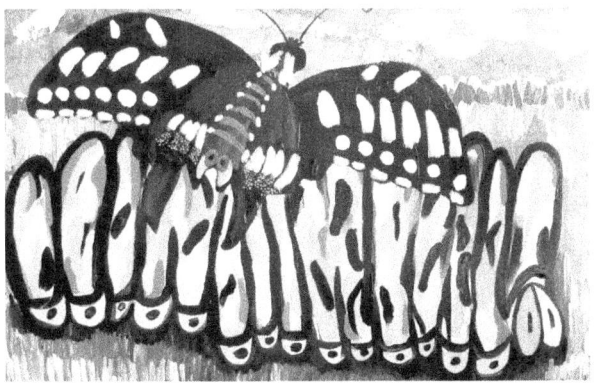

I Know Dan, Not Everything Texas is Fear and Misogyny 2015. Acrylic on Masonite®, 20 x 13"

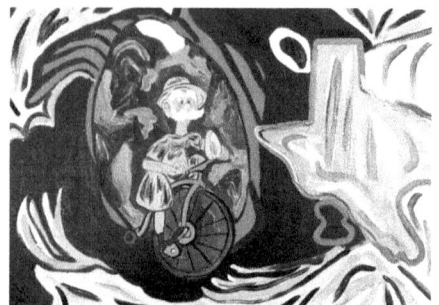

Dan's Favorite Toy On Earth 2015. Acrylic on Masonite®, 20 x 13"

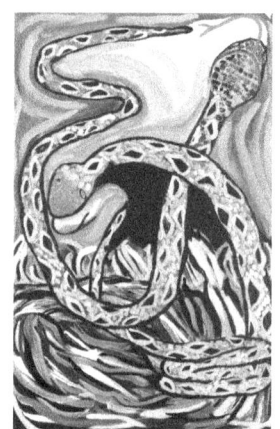

Diamondback Water Snakes Have Been Recorded Breeding in Texas
2015. Acrylic on Masonite®, 13 x 20"

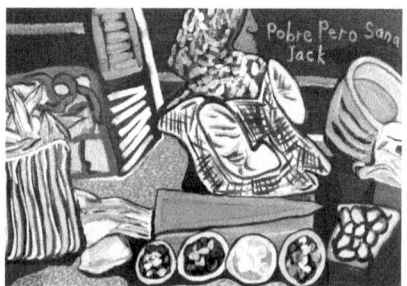

Dan Photographed Mexico in 1983 2015. Acrylic on Masonite®, 20 x 13"

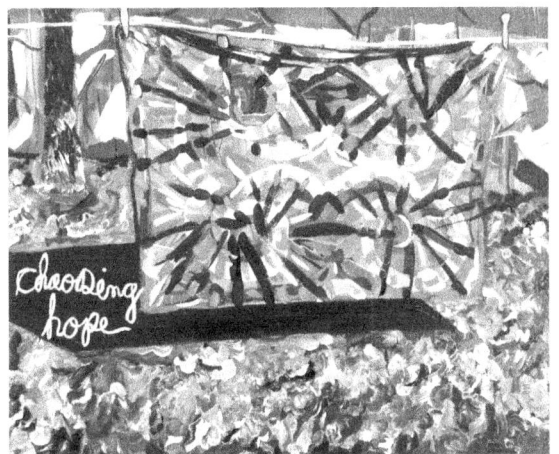

Chaosing Hope 2015. Acrylic on canvas 20 x 16"

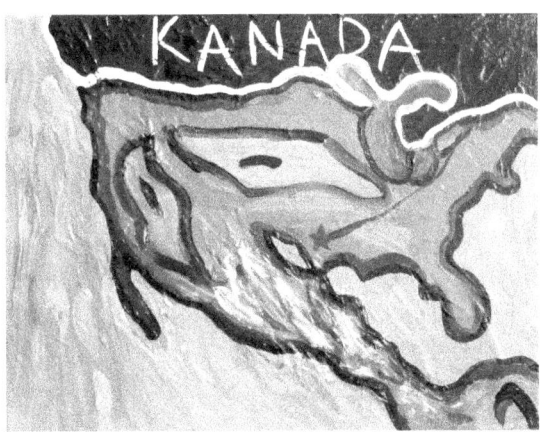

Kanada is Dreamy in February 2015. Acrylic on canvas, 10 x 8"

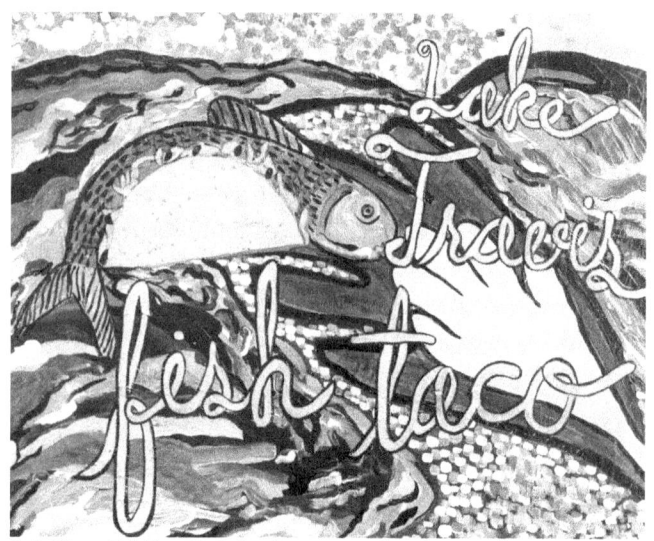

Lake Travis Fish Taco 2015. Acrylic on canvas board, 20 x 16"

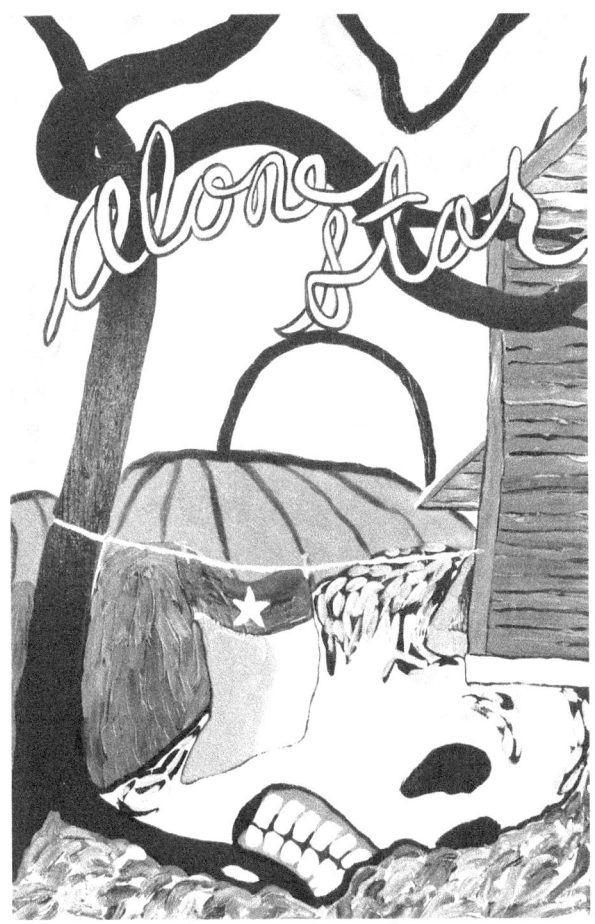

Alone Star 2015. Acrylic on Masonite®, 13 x 20"

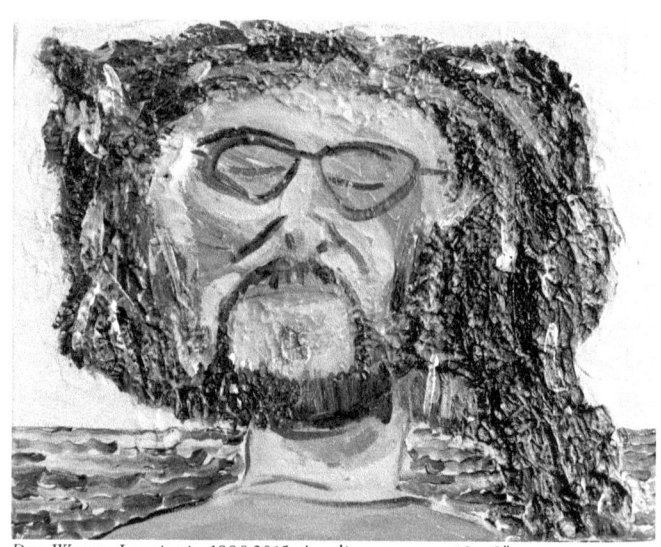

Dan Went to Jamaica in 1980 2015. Acrylic on canvas, 10 x 8"

Bye Dan

I believe I am finished with the "Dan" series. Looking forward to the party. My paintings will go cheaper than a crate of pumpkins. It's the way of the world. Dan will get a couple fill-ups of gas, after I have spent a few hundred hours amassing 2-D color for a good time. Music, country wines, summer—an all day goodbye to a dear friend. Us fools certainly know what good nonsense is. And we revere it with the joyous anticipation of lovers.

I began these on April 1st, or thereabouts. An appropriate fool's attempt at acquiring a small fortune for our friend before he embarks on the greatest odyssey ever known. The silent auction will be a great success. The titles are printed on a handout, and next to each one is a number referring to a specific reserve marker. That means, no bids below the designation, por favor.

1. A fast food stop for Dan and son $16
2. A campsite for the night and one bundle of firewood $26.00
3. A full tank of unleaded gasoline plus two bottled waters and muffin for Rufus $36

Also, Dan has graciously offered a bottle of his country wine for any painting that brings in over $35

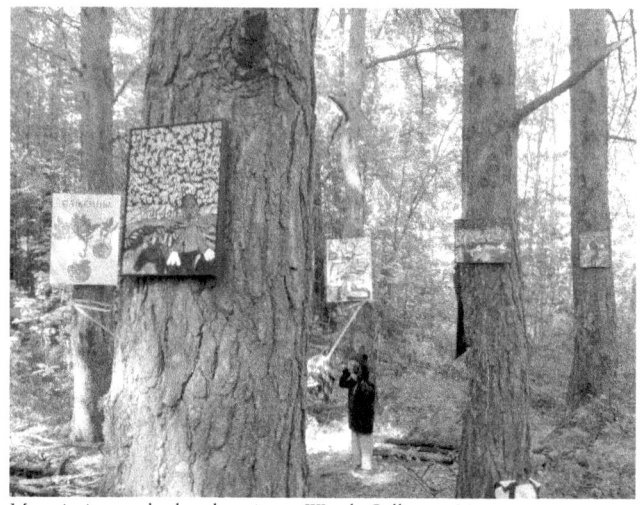

My paintings and others hanging at Woods Gallery in Moscow

Ha! Take that ubiquitous, flowing artist resumes of avarice! Thanks to Alexey Stepanov of Moscow, Russia, I am an international painter. Also, a thank you to Russia whose mothers have raised boys and girls to discover the art of dreaming. Who would guess that painters are the same everywhere, true painters, the non-misanthropic ones, who aren't finished yet nurturing their humanity.

Some points from the Stuckism Manifesto:

Stuckism is the quest for authenticity. By removing the mask of cleverness and admitting where we are, the Stuckist allows him/herself uncensored expression.

It is the most difficult task of all. The art crazy old man knows.

I have been in love with painting ever since I became conscious of it at the age of six. I drew some pictures I thought fairly good when I was fifty, but really nothing I did before the age of seventy was of any value at all. At seventy-three I have at least caught every aspect of nature–birds, fish, animals, insects, trees, grasses, all. When I am eighty I shall have developed still further and I will really master the secrets of art at ninety. when I reach a hundred my work will be truly sublime and my final goal will be attained around the age of one hundred and ten, when every line and dot I draw will be imbued with life.—from Hokusai's "The Art Crazy Old Man"

The Stuckist is not mesmerized by the glittering prizes, but is wholeheartedly engaged in the process of painting. Success to the Stuckist is to get out of bed in the morning and paint.

Tell that to slave master billionaire art collectors Paul Allen and David Geffen, men of the abstract wealth — a watered-down, water-logged, soaked socks, silly concept of abstract wealth.

The ego-artist's constant striving for public recognition results in a constant fear of failure. The Stuckist risks failure willfully and mindfully by daring to transmute his/her ideas through the realms of painting. Whereas the ego-artist's fear of failure inevitably brings about an underlying self-loathing, the failures that the Stuckist encounters engage him/her in a deepening process which leads to the understanding of the futility of all striving. The Stuckist doesn't strive — which is to avoid who and where you are — the Stuckist engages with the moment.

I am still caught up in the romantic's dream. It comes and goes. I apply to art houses, magazines, Internet blogs to show work with the hopes that my ship will come in. Granted it's a poverty canoe like Picasso's. He wanted to be rich to live like a pauper. I want to sell paintings in order to live like a pauper in a garret on a Grecian island, always with more paint and whole foods. At times the path may appear to be hyper vanity, but when I reach deeper, it is understood that the queries, exposure, sometimes outright begging is just the ancient human quest for authenticity unto the clan.

It is the Stuckist's duty to explore his/her neurosis and innocence through the making of paintings and displaying them in public, thereby enriching society by giving shared form to individual experience and an individual form to shared experience.

We are mere fools an ocean apart. The woods in Russia where 21st century painters meet. No money here. No good things for you to see, pampered sissies of New York. Go cuddle up in your cult of personality pillows!

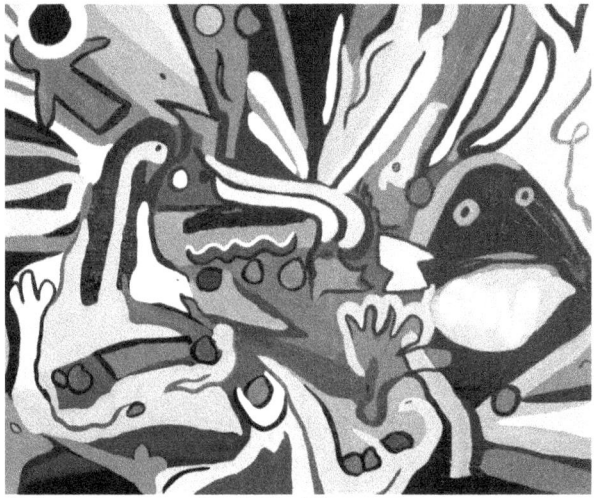

2015. Acrylic on canvas board, 24 x 18"

Painstakingly De-plinked From Their Sprays

Finally, thank you Hyperallergic for seeing into the future. Keep up the good work. Posting an example of painters beginning again where the 19th century Paris cafes left off, can remind enough people in a day that art is human—precisely not business, not economic bubble, not New York, not gallery, not celebrity, not factory, not drone, not black SUV, not hallmark holiday, not football team, not sheik, not soccer mom, not checkbook, not Internet, not smartphone, not plastic wrap, not new age, not live and let live, not notness, and definitely certainly not misanthropy on the tip top tippy-top not of the not, not, not, not, knotty-not not scale.

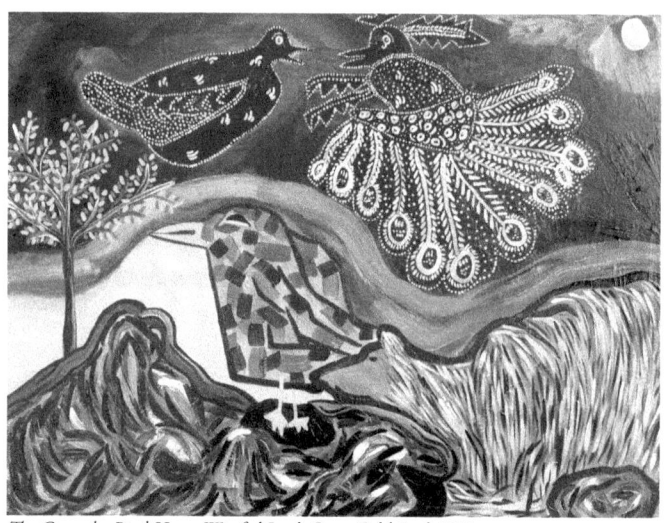

The Gouache Bird Has a Wistful Look On a Cold Rock 2015.
Acrylic on canvas, 24 x 18"

The Price List Introduction From My Last Show:

Okay. I must disclose this.

I am a terrible failure at making money.

I can't even barter well. In the past I have asked for olive oil, chain saw lessons, French wine—it is nigh impossible to wrestle money, or even goods, for art out of normal people of modest means. I even offered to trade a painting at my last show to anyone willing to say "Ron Throop, great painter" daily for one month to different people each time. I feel rotten pricing anything, but know that ArtRage cannot continue indefinitely to provide quality shows with food and flowers without bones thrown to administration once in a while.

Therefore I have priced these works at the cost to my wife, who supports my acrylic painting habit, with an added 40% of bones with meat still left on for ArtRage. I charge $10/hour for my time. I have eliminated my usual 30% element "X" fee added to time and cost of materials. The element "X" fee, also known as "fool's buck", is that portion of total cost that compensates beyond what repeated narcissistic failure can appropriate to any idiot with a free hand. Please reach into your wallets and support ArtRage. The money I make will not help my future so much as to pay a debt to my past. I know there is value to any Throop you purchase today. At 48 years of age, I have a clean bill of health and a work ethic that would make John Calvin shame-faced so much to lock his own head in the pillory. I will continue to produce like a hummingbird on speed. I will not die until Rose (my wife) has an archive that will give her a big fat bargaining chip for her next husband to salivate over. If a painting you like is out of your range, please buy a book, or ask me to jig for nickels (ArtRage will still get its cut).

Thank you.

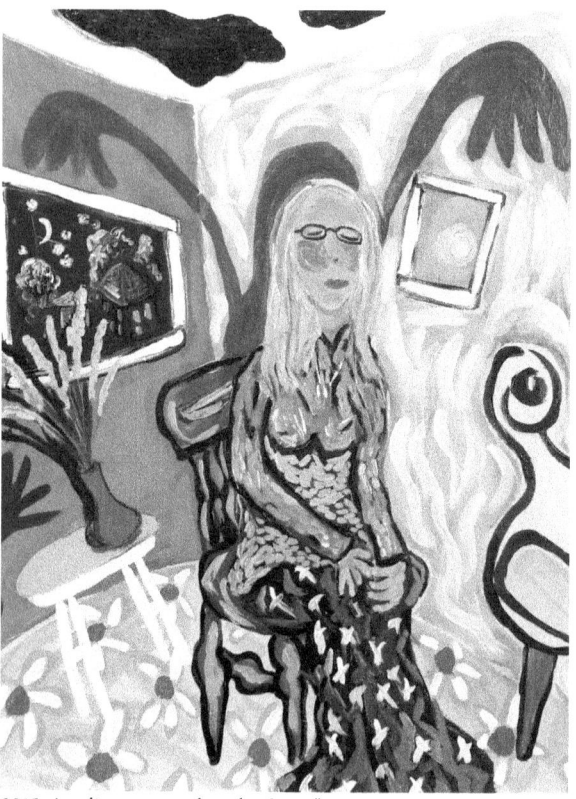

2015. Acrylic on canvas board, 16 x 20"

The Fabric Artist

A commission! Paint any theme I like about an old friend for eight bottles of country wine. I know the berries that were picked. I feel the sweat and mosquitoes, the single torturous deer fly, the de-plinking of elderberries, burning blackberry bush thorn stabs in the fingers and thumbs... There is no doubt about it—I got the better deal.

The painting depicts a mutual friend, a famous fabric artist living in Texas. She used to be my neighbor in New York. Before that, she lived in Taos, New Mexico. And before that, the Rocky Mountains of Colorado. She's back in the Lone Star state where she was born and raised. The prodigal daughter. She meditates on her demons, but like all of humanity over the age of 22, they never ever go away.

She and Dan, the commissioner of this painting, used to live together. I was very moved by their hand-to-mouth artistic lifestyle. One day I painted the following to celebrate their togetherness.

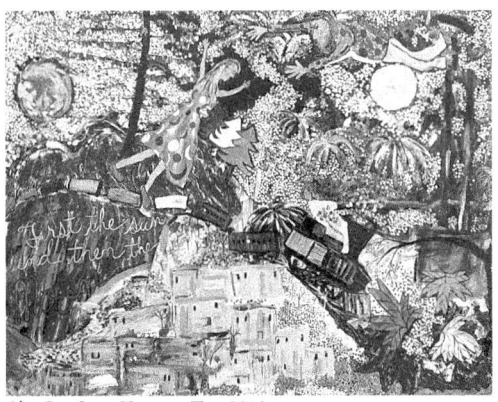

She Got On a Train in Taos 2013.
Acrylic on panel board, 64 x 48"

They are not together anymore. This painting dry rots in my basement studio. It is a piece of their history before the love shack caved in. Who could blame either of them? They built paradise from the top down.

Henry Thoreau, the unloved bachelor of nature science, on jaded love:

If you have built castles in the air, your work need not be lost; that is where they should be. Now put the foundations under them.

I wish them both discovery of the permanence of love in Texas. It is the great mind regulator. Which reminds me of a quote from another Henry, a modern unloved bachelor of nihilism science:

It was the door called death which always swung open, and I saw that there was no death, nor were there any judges or executioners save in our imagining. How desperately I strove to make restitution! And I did make restitution. Full and complete. The rajah stripping himself naked. Only an ego left, but an ego puffed and swollen like a hideous toad. And then the utter insanity of it would overwhelm me. Nothing can be given or taken away; nothing has been added or subtracted; nothing increased or diminished. We stand on the same shore before the same mighty ocean. The ocean of love. There it is—in perpetuum. As much in a broken blossom, the sound of a waterfall, the swoop of a carrion bird, as in the thunderous artillery of the prophet. We move with eyes shut and ears stopped. We smash walls where doors are waiting to open at the touch; we grope for ladders, forgetting that we have wings; we pray as if God were deaf and blind, as if He were in space. No wonder the angels in our midst are unrecognizable...

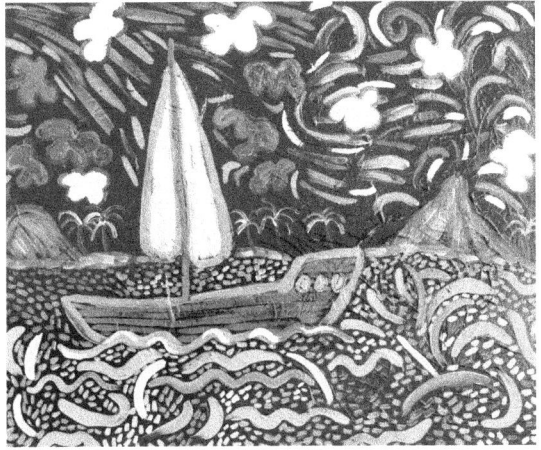

2015. Acrylic on canvas board, 20 x 16"

Application of Minimalistic Whimsy To Wet Black Canvas, Setting Stroke Capacity at 5,000

This began as a student throw-away canvas board that my friend Dan the professor dropped off with others. My first attempt was to capture my wife's gentle spirit in a portrait of her. Covered. Second attempt, a wild, dark three cup-of-coffee abstract. Covered again in black. Finally, the child Ronnie's boat anchored at sea waking up to a gentle volcano. From the top of my esophagus, across the upper chest and arms, I sometimes feel the overwhelming urge to turn the apparatus inside-out and scrape back deeply to the skin— there is that much muddy mix to unload. Ah! But to paint again clean, fresh and free. To begin again. To be born again. That is the meaning of paint!

Meanwhile, another failure to behold.

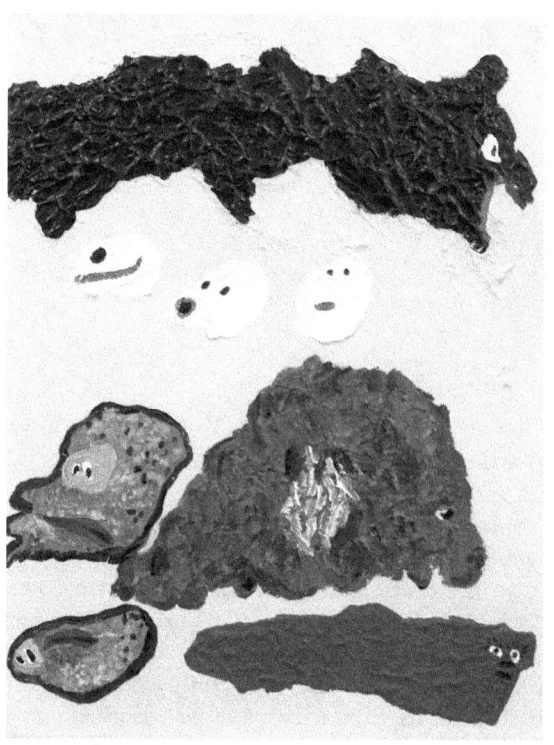

2015. Acrylic on canvas, 11 x 14"

Natural Resources Regroup After Humanity Stops Buggering One Another

I have been bike riding to the local library with my daughter several days this week. She to the costume design and drawing books. Me to the painters. I don't think my research is healthy. I pick a painter that I feel my limitations could compare to, yet after skimming through a few pages, I am usually unseated from the lounge chair in awe and wonder. The 20th century moderns were following a pattern. Most of their younger work is highly skilled in constipated rendering. Then, maybe a several year phase in abstract, mixed in with a looser expressionism. And finally, freedom and joy, perhaps even so confident as to present a colored cartoon at the salon. Some influential photographer is there to help the painter make history. Often with another famous artist(s) beside him, both photographed in three-piece suits, smoking cigarettes, and all of them men. Caucasian men.

What the majority of these celebrity painters share in common, post-van Gogh, is recognition in youth and geography. The former fueled their next painting. Encouragement (plus food and raiment) kept the painter painting, and not seeking an alternative career in furniture sales. The latter was (is) all about being in the right place at the right time, amidst a big city art media that "makes" the artist, similar to the arbitrary growth of institutions like religion and federal buildings. None of the established modern greats have painted in the middle of nowhere anonymously. Some lucky outsiders get recognition in very old age, or more likely after death, to the banking joys of posterity. But the overall pattern is this: young painter in big city winning critical praise with inspired work, getting paid in actual money or status, and enjoying self pride and encouragement unto the next studio output. It's what I call the *Bob Dylan of success as an artist paradigm*. Without early Greenwich Village accolades, Bob would have packed his dufflebag and got on a Greyhound bus back to Hibbing, Minnesota. Maybe, if brave, he would have stayed in New York to work a job in the service industry, and while young, continue to search for that "big break". Eventually, after repeated failure, he would settle in with a girl, find more secure employment, get married, go suburb, raise children, etc. By wild chance, Dylan won New York status while very young, was fueled exponentially thereafter, and like all lifelong successful 20th century artists, was promoted. Of course Dylan worked very hard each day to create beautiful stuff shared with an earth of eager human admirers. Yet without initial success and popular geography, no promoter (Columbia Records) would risk the initial investment.

Now pride dictates to me, the painter, that I shun the parties and the "glittering prizes" that the Stuckists are wont to do. That is just financial failure speaking in its best cognitive dissonance accent. I will never become the tiniest fraction of success of brand Bob Dylan, who, now in his wiser old age, probably would also yearn for the wisdom of obscurity. But as a young man, Dylan was an eager, very talented, lowly prostitute working the New York streets and clubs, and not much more than that. The band wagon picked him up, and couldn't stop. Compare the Bob Dylan story to all famous 20th century painters in their more humble, varying degrees of celebrity. I would argue that the similarities are too real to ignore.

So, finally, in desperation, Throop calls out to star-makers of the 21st century and its plucky Internet. Partake in my eBay auction to undermine the archaic 20th century law of financial stability for artists. Buy inspired art that cannot carry the blue-ribbon of critical praise and big city geography. It has no clout. It is nothing but a man, made up of so many elements and minerals.

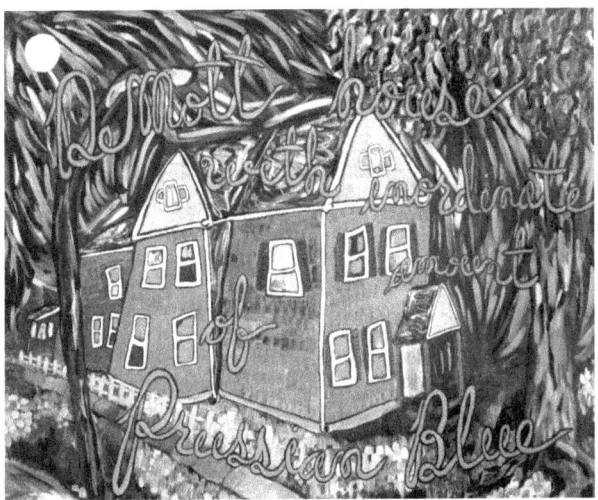

2015. Acrylic on canvas 30 x 24"

Demott House

A friend of mine liked my idea of painters trading their work, in order to keep the business of art less fretful. Who better than a painter to revere the colored rectangle of another? I'll appreciate his or her time and effort, and I don't have to feel "taken" in a world gone so wrong that for many, buying Twix Bars® in bulk poses no existential irony, yet to think about trusting oneself to have private, subjective taste, followed by a purchase of a stranger's art, is so uncomfortable as to be practically obscene. Just take a walk throughout an American home and ask the resident to point out the original art purchased without pity. You might have to climb over a pile of forgotten garage sale country crafts in the basement before stumbling upon one true expression by a human being not of the family clan.

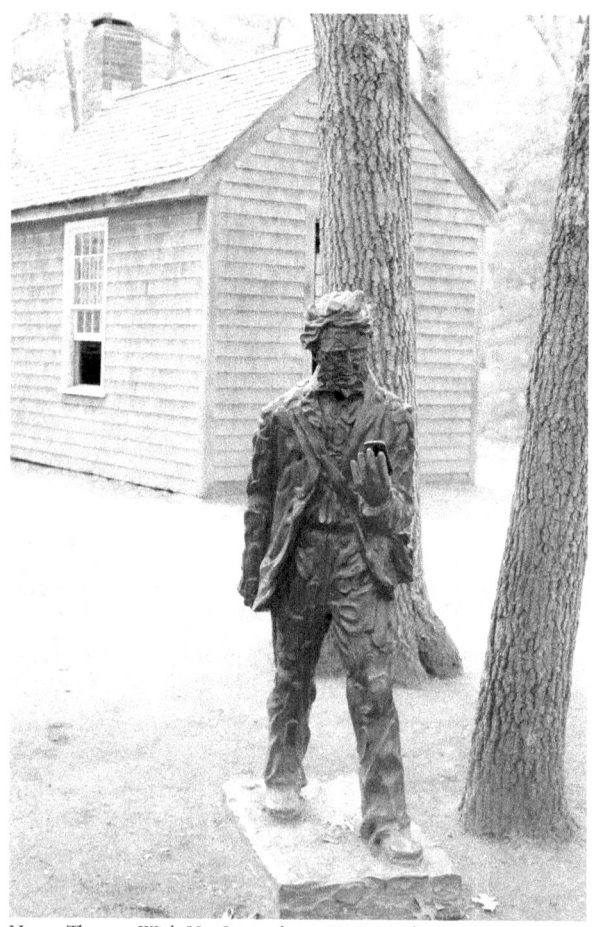

Henry Thoreau With His Smartphone 2015. Acrylic on canvas board, 16 x 20"

The Past Is My Future at Walden Pond

For two years Henry David Thoreau lived in a tiny house he built on the northern shore of Walden Pond. He was a philosopher who, like everyone else, ate and slept and voided excrement, but unlike anyone these days, drafted a life worth living to a nineteenth century humanity rife with bacteria and virus that did not play nice. In my opinion, the memory of his fingernail dirt has more value on the exchange market of a modern earth turning than the life of any president or prime minister. He could conduct a future rife with wisdom to any poor boy in America over the age of eleven while wrapped up for a day in his great coat. Thoreau— a higher prince than a modern Buddha, less of a dandy than flutey Krishna, and all the glory Jesus would have become if Texas never happened. I shall not explain, but I will tell you. I am weary of all interpretation and attempts at persuasion. As of today I have transformed into the 21st century mutant red squirrel chip-monk. My eyes won't blink. I distrust all several billion of you. Your species is insane. Without reason and philosophy, all people are suspect in a culture of sun and moon chasing unto death.

Slip on your tights and bike ride to cleanse, thin middle-aged men of America. There's a good work-out waiting. Climb a mountain, kayak a pond, check your heart and pulse rates with a magic watch fat burger automatons, and order bean sprouts to sweep out those greasy prostates.

Look what Americans have done to the memory of a great man! A state park. Ten bucks a car. Hired summer work to take the money, but no one paid to love the park. The bike riders come, with bike and gear worth more at resale than all I have accumulated in coin thus far with creative effort. Working class swimmers climbing out from their railroad shanties at midday to test their pallid potato skins in the broad daylight. No proud gait. No soft eyes. Smart-phoning selfies while the Fitchburg railroad roars past the southwestern shoreline. In the guest book at Thoreau's model cabin a girl wrote "Your book sucked". I wrote beside her name, "iPhone® thug!" Obviously a young girl, forced to read *Walden* in high school English class. A breathing, walking mound of ignorance—the embodiment of failure of parents and teachers unschooled in humility, reverence, and pride. The poor girl doesn't have a chance at happiness and will die a theoretical old maid with the latest game app glued to her face. We handed the bronze statue Henry our Tracfone® and told him to GPS the Marlboro Road. Oops, the data was maxed. So he opted to snort a rock of meth on the pond beach with wannabe Boston skinheads and compare stupid tattoos.

We made our way to the pond and walked north along the shoreline. A man in full body American flag swimsuit was divulging his daily hair gel routine to two interested men obviously unhappy enough about their own hair to commit homicide. At that moment I wanted war to rain down upon us. There can be no future for my unborn grandchildren if this kind of narcissism has reached Walden Pond en masse. Just a few paces more and we arrived at the cabin site, the only original construction left being the foundation to the fireplace. Some society in 1947 thought enough of Thoreau to memorialize it for future Walden perambulators. I am grateful. I touched the stone that Henry dragged to this spot like a believer of the Dark Ages stroked a traveling sandal strap facsimile of his beloved savior. Humility revered is a wonderful feeling. It is a human touch we need now more than ever. So rare is it to be found in this present society. No one lauds the greatness of others in order to mark a hopeful destination for themselves. A woman came up with her friend and I overheard her telling him that living at Walden was no big deal; Thoreau brought his laundry to his mother. Can't be a great thinker if someone does your laundry! The arrogant ignorance of my countrymen. This poor woman can't breathe without Ronald McDonald®, gasoline, French cheese, Vietnam sweatshops, Proctor and Gamble®, Internet connection, smart phone, 20% gratuity, big media everything, alarm clock snooze and periodontics unto death after partial.

Up on "Author's Ridge", back in Concord village, Emerson self combusted his bones after hearing that one. Alcott didn't get the irony—she always did her man's laundry... And wrote books. Equality she knew was seven generations or more away, so adversity was obvious and had to be overcome. Now thoughtful people leave trinkets at her grave, and dumb people piss their Pepsi® in Walden Pond. Thoreau's mother did his laundry! My god, we should just start eating each other if this is what humanity has become in Concord, Massachusetts. Arrogant ignorance. Men teaching men about hair gel products. Dogs being invited to shop with their loved ones. Bicycling for no other reason than to detox almonds, kale, and the occasional meat product prepared by immigrant slaves a thousand miles away. Target® probably sells "Civil Disobedience". Why not? It's all cuckoo without men like Thoreau. America had a very brief Greek revival in a time of devastating child mortality and over-the-top fear of the supernatural. So brief that it lost all ground after one generation. Thoreau knew what seeds his contemporaries would leave. He wrote warnings and solutions. At the Old North Bridge that is in need of much care, the grounds being neglected from lack of help, one can look skyward to a machine of war flying by. It's good and loud—both arrogant and ignorant. Back home the pilot gels his hair and learns from his kids a new smart phone app. This weekend the family is taking the bikes up to Newburyport to ride the bay circuit to Ipswich. About as transcendental as Gandhi on a lunchbox, or Martin Luther King boulevard on a hot summer day.

Henry Thoreau lived for me, but only I can give a damn.

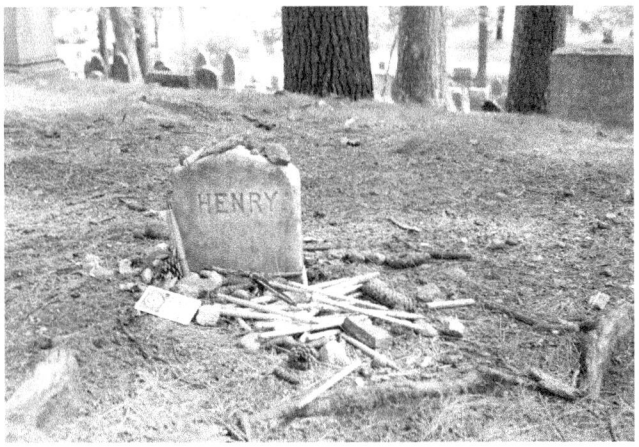

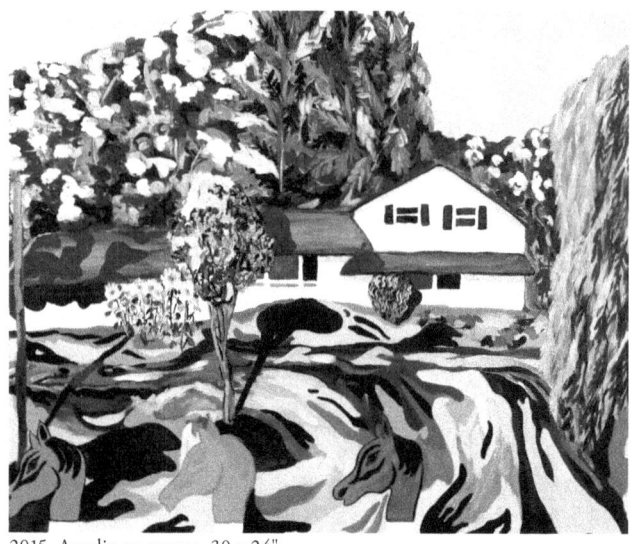
2015. Acrylic on canvas, 30 x 24"

Olson House

This will show Friday night at my local art association. How difficult to sell a painting just hoping to buy more paints. I must turn on the autobiography full force, at any expense, and no looking back. I am the only one buying it, and now I believe this is the best way through. Archive my life visually; at times literally. No one is paying attention but love, and as any mammal besides human already knows, there is no other way.

Wake. Paint. Meditate. Nurture. Think. Love. Eat. Sleep. Wake.

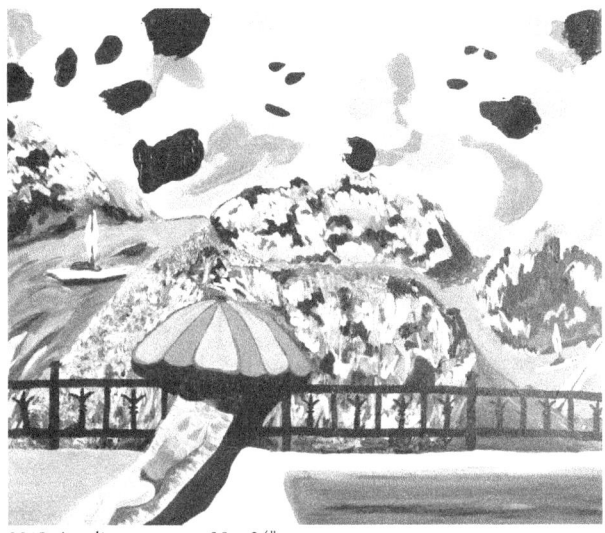

2015. Acrylic on canvas, 30 x 24"

Spending Pretend Money In Bar Harbor, Maine

A Painter or poet can find time to "spend it all" too. He must economize all year and vacation with dread buffers stuffed deep into his ears. It's a tough fight with oneself, but in the end, well worth the irrational battle. Why anyone would read the biographies of spoiled children like Lord Byron or Shelly will always be a mystery to me. They could not have known happiness. Not with all that boredom! I'll allow Whitman the last word:

Sometimes With Money I Love

Sometimes with money I love I fill myself with worry for fear of it,
But now I think there is no reason to be afraid, the payback is
certain one way or another
(I loved a certain currency ardently and my love was never re
turn'd,
Yet out of that I have painted these pictures).

by Waltron Whitman

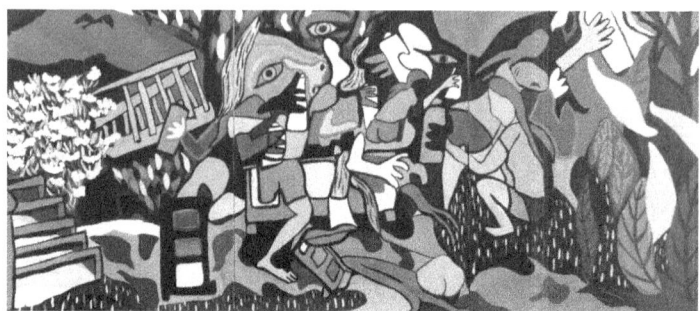

2015. Acrylic on canvas, (3) 11 x 14"

Rose Spray Painting Old Window Seat

Well, it's official. I need drawing lessons. I sat by the tobacco and sketched while my wife attacked a furniture reject she found at a dumpster. She knows how to draw and also put harmony back on track. Not me. I practice my limitations daily and dream way too much. Still, after each failure, I always make sure to color it in! Fools can have virtue too, you know... After they finish. I can't draw, but with decent preservation, I bet our great grandkids will hang this on their wall one day, and tell visitors their own story of us. A long time after the fake Internet archive is dead.

A good Saturday morning to pull garlic and weed around the edible weeds. And I have promised my wife that I'll keep the pencil at bay.

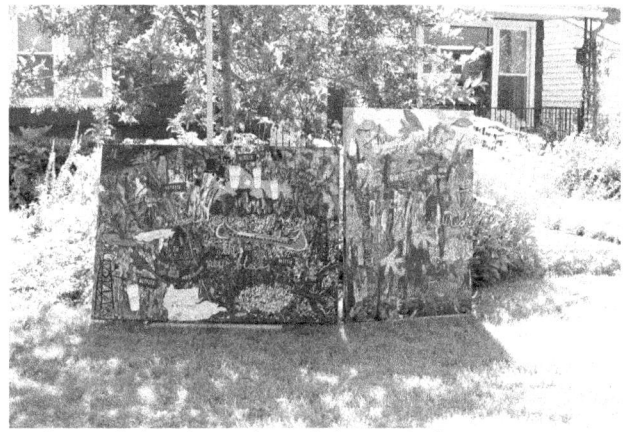

My front yard where the art of perambulation is dead.

The business of art is an oxymoron fit for a moron lemonade stand, yet I keep at it, like a duck addicted to quack. Why not? The work trucks pass by with Taylor Swift sound ripples on the wind, as the squirrels re-discover their nuts in the artist garden. There is always hope, and therein lies happiness. Cha-ching! Gagosian the elder discovered me while I was taking out the trash. He asked if I could pencil in a few weeks this fall for a Paris show. I told him flat out "No", that he'll have to wait in line behind the family out bike riding their safety helmets and the multiple heart attack man counting his strokes on a fast walk to another dinner of cheese and white bread.

Painters stop, go. No one is buying. No one at all. Can you hear the poleese siren? Cops are kicking the crap out of enthusiasm down on Highway 61.

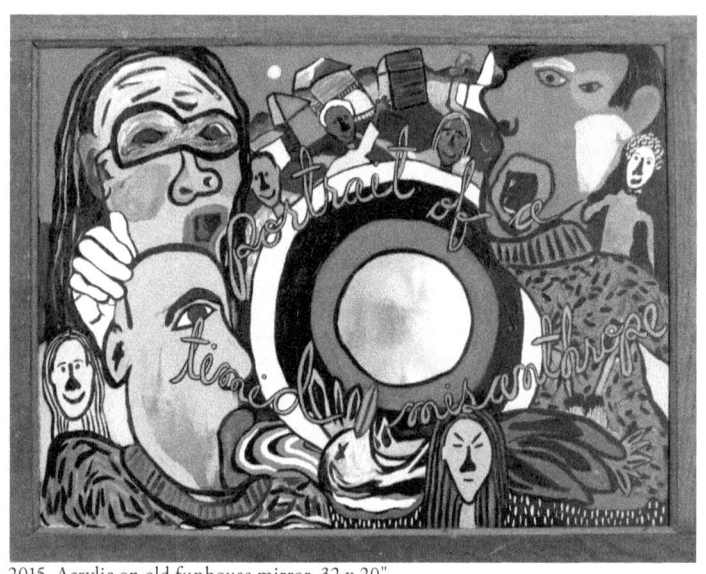

2015. Acrylic on old funhouse mirror, 32 x 20"

Portrait of a Timid Misanthrope

Painting on a mirror, even one that's clear gessoed, can be frustrating on a humid day. It doesn't like to be touched. Too many strokes and its glass shines through. This will hang next week in a portrait gallery show. You can look at it and see the real you among humanity. To the modern misanthrope, which I surmise is most everyone over age fifteen, people appear approachable, maybe even friendly, from a distance. However, move close enough to depict their eye color, and become afraid instantly. Immediate fight or flight in expression or deed. Not saying "Hello" to a fellow passerby on the sidewalk portrays the inner dread we all possess at the thought of letting our guard down to a stranger. Of course it all depends on location. Very few of us fear the cashier at the super-duper market, or any established institution that sells things to us. Then it's a matter of justifiable power over another. Fear is lifted, and we temporarily bask in an 11th century Japanese court of politeness and respect.

This painting reminds me of the second to last paragraph in Henry Miller's Tropic of Cancer:

Human beings make a strange fauna and flora. From a distance they appear negligible; up close they are apt to appear ugly and malicious. More than anything they need to be surrounded with sufficient space—space even more than time.

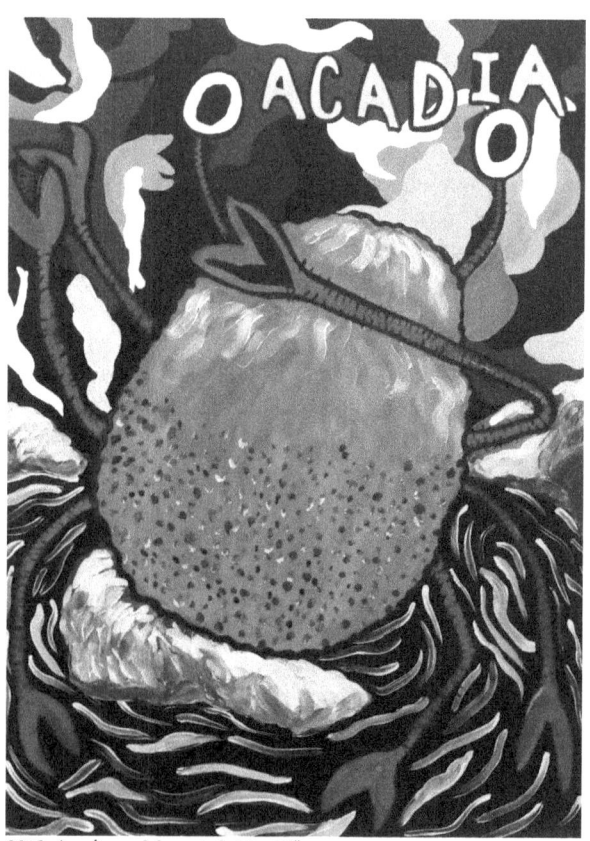

2015. Acrylic on Masonite®, 12 x 16"

In Acadia You Weren't Pregnant, and I Couldn't Draw a Crab in Existence

There you have it! The worst drawing ever of a crab by a man who would sell you a painting with only a slight blush. It's what comes out of a non-photogenic mind while sketching dreams in a 5 x 7" travel log. The other night I was called a fauvist at a gallery opening. The woman likened me to André Duran, who I never heard of, but told her the name would be easy to remember. Duran—half the name in my wife's favorite childhood rock band. And André— a cheap New Year's Eve sparkling wine. I'll look him up now... Okay, it's André Derain, and he was a Fauvist, although in the photography, he looks more tame than a collie. I would think a wild beast to look more like this:

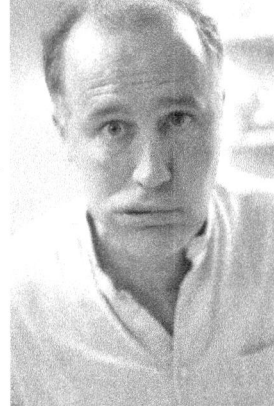

Me pretending to be a
steam locomotive

It was a kind compliment, but dead wrong.

Therefore, to better define my style for the critics, whose silence is deafening, I need to name my movement. I'll put it in a romantic tongue to give it some posh, and hope that most people forking over dough for my work don't speak Spanish.

Los Tontos Aficionados. That is, those of us who paint every-day, over many years time, and never get paid, yet still do it. That is, persisting in our folly, hoping to become wise, but really just persisting in our folly. And some of us think crabs have strands of skin covered sinew with eyeballs bobbling on top.

The amateur fools!

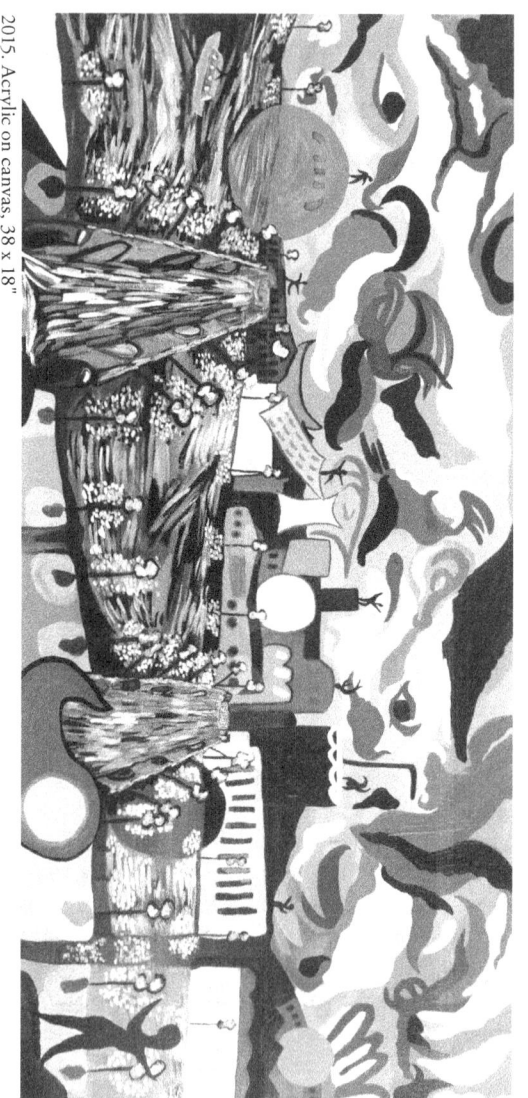

2015. Acrylic on canvas, 38 x 18"

I Want To Paint in a City That Needs Artists and Clowns

I'll know I have painted my own perfection the morning I can tell my wife, as we sip coffee in the window chair, that I have achieved the magic breeze, and sent the latest piece back to from where it came. The day I approach a blank canvas with the same confidence a journeyman plumber tightens a sink drain will be fine, yes, and may come in my lifetime. The magic breeze I am talking about visited the modern masters, van Gogh, Picasso, Philp Guston even... I am confident I could define it, if it ever came. Rembrandt? Velasquez? No magic breeze for them, nor anyone who painted for the pleasures of royalty or aspirations to universal perfection. They painted everyday with the constipation of desiring super-humanity, as if almost to declare another species unto themselves, while pleasing their commission, their patron merchant or king. Compared to today, try making a painting that would please the likes of a George W. Bush. One would have to sleep on a bed of used hot dogs for a month, bathe in chimichanga sauce, moan low over a toilet bowl, to finally produce a LeRoy Neiman horse-being-gelded masterpiece.

The modern masters felt the freedom enter their toes and flow through their bodies and out their eyeballs like spirit magic. I know it because I "feel" what needs to happen, but a guillotine slams the toe tunnel shut every time. And I paint with an increasing tightening in my forearms. The evening I finish a piece, raise a glass of blackberry wine to it, take it from the easel, hug it to my chest, run to the lake bluff to finally frisbee it off back to god... Then I know I will have achieved the satori of modern masterhood. Where will I be? When will it happen? I sure as hell won't be on the Internet to yarn about it. Probably postmortem, as the wife frisbees my ashes off the lake bluff to Canada.

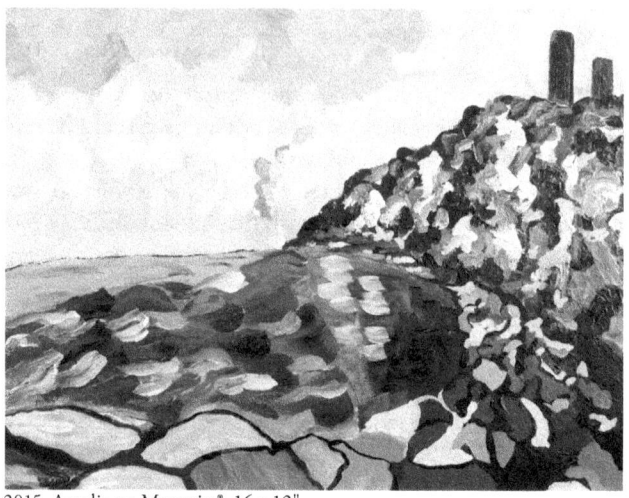

2015. Acrylic on Masonite®, 16 x 12"

Matisse Was Right In Matters of Joy and Toasting Success

I need to explain the genesis of this painting. It began in my mind long before brush touched board—actually, at dusk the day before I got up from bed on a harried-to-be morning with my plein air materials set at the door ready to go. I would teach myself to paint in the light of day. A month or two, whatever it took of daily jaunts out into nature to record what I sat down to see—my eyes, arm and left hand making interpretive copy of what was already right there in front of me. I walked down to the lake like an intense van Gogh, but unlike him in so many ways as to render me the most simpleton fool tool to the greatest of painting's idiots. I set up on the rocks and commenced painting the view. I wish I had a picture snapped behind me. What was coming out on the canvas looked very similar to this photo taken last year.

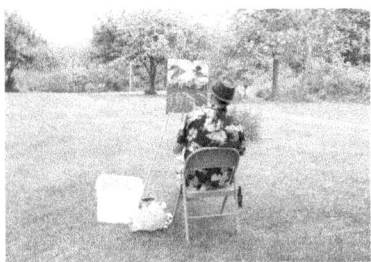

I was set up outside on a beautiful spring day intent on painting my wish to keep the rain at bay. There is an expression from days gone by that if you can throw a cat through the clouds, then it will not rain. Meaning that somebody's great great aunt heard that if a cat can fit inside a patch of blue sky, then she would not have to take an umbrella to the county fair.

My attempt in the photo didn't last much longer. Seconds after the picture was taken I brushed over the board in heavy grays and black. I didn't feel good about painting what I saw. So I finished the day enjoying the outdoors with my family and friends, and went home thinking of weather folklore. The next day in the studio I set up the largest canvas available and for the next week, commenced painting with my thoughts and only what the canvas beheld in front of me. Here is the result:

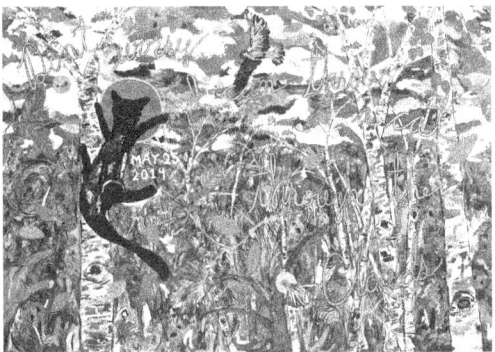

Don't Worry, I Can Throw a Cat Through the Clouds 2015.
Acrylic on canvas, 73x 54"

I had no luck in the wild, but was thoroughly satisfied "working in the head," abiding by my own genius.

This finished painting was the forth attempt to paint a scene I saw on Monday morning. While at the rock beach, painting the view, I had three unremarkable failures. I could have titled them: *Straining, Impotence,* and *Self-doubt.* For the rest of the day I felt awful, a great sham, a delusion unto myself, and a guilty criminal to loved ones who believe in me. What a heavy load. I scribbled the board in grays and blacks, and laid off painting for a day in order to follow through with promised summer chores, thinking often about my failure. And then at some point the following afternoon, Matisse popped into my head. Rather, words once uttered by him. I paraphrase: "I don't paint what I see as much as what is in my mind." Then a mantra silently repeated over and over again while making dinner, visiting with the family, and finally settling down on a hot night.

Up in the morning, down to the studio. I could not paint fast enough the scene of a couple days ago. Plein air just doesn't work out for me. Maybe nature is what it is and only some form of torture can come to those who attempt imitation. I would rather paint the cat with a red halo being thrown out to the clouds, than struggle with strokes that make me feel like I'm having a stroke. So finally I can say after many years time, in matters of plein air painting, I know what I do not know, and that is a milestone joy worth toasting a glass to. Here's to you Mr. Matisse!

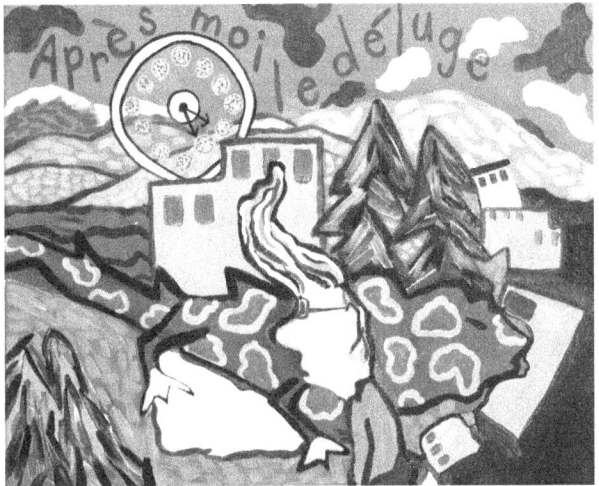

2015. Acrylic on canvas, 14 x 11"

Dan Is Nearly Religious Pizza

Several interpretations on the Internet for the painted French phrase translated, "After me, the flood". I just opened up a phrase book and came across it in the "A's". With a little bit of imagination, I have made it fit in the painting. My friend Dan is on the move and rekindling his faith in humanity. From cooped up winter garret rat, to expressive, free-born man-becoming-native-again through romantic love, Dan is vicariously proving to me the power of polite push-back upon an atomizing new age. He is an anomaly, an aristocrat of the spirit, settling for what could be forever, or just another live long day in the high desert.

Why didn't they leave us to wander through buttercup summers?
Why didn't they leave us to wander when there was no other?

—Van Morrison

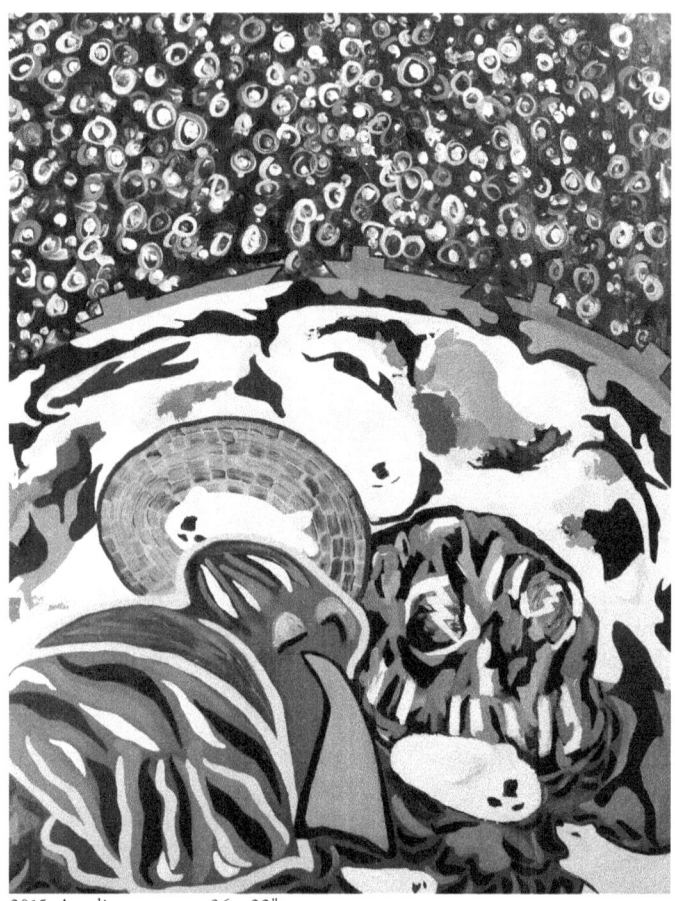

2015. Acrylic on canvas, 36 x 22"

Teardrop, the Flightless Arctic Bird, Hopes a Robert Peary Meteorite Kidney Stone Lodged in the Urinary Tracts of All G8 Leaders

A very long title. Sometimes the message is the medium. Otherwise the painting looks like a bunch of lounging seals on Armageddon holiday with "iron ships on the water, very free... and easy".

No, Teardrop understands the chemistry of water, its four states on earth—liquid, solid, gas, and drowning. She knows where the last iron meteorite of Northern Greenland resides, and before its ice carpet is pulled out from under it, she hopes to magically reproduce the huge rock eight times inside the urinary tracts of the great G8.

Who are these bozos determining the fates of species? Good grandparents? Humble pilgrims? Humans are always so pathetically busy being human—all eight nations were blowing up multiple trillions of fauna and flora just two generations ago. And they are still able to hold earth in a vice. My God, for being such perfect losers, they sure have a lot of pull! Even after several hundred years with dominion over earth, they are powerless to inflict widespread contentment upon their own species. I think Teardrop and her friends know what's going on, and they're not gonna wait for Marvin Gaye to deliver the message this era. I'll watch the cramping agony on Swiss time at the next G8 summit. After a giant meteorite bursts out of eight leaders at once, it will be very difficult to persuade replacements.

Hooray! Earth as it was when being human did not matter to anything.

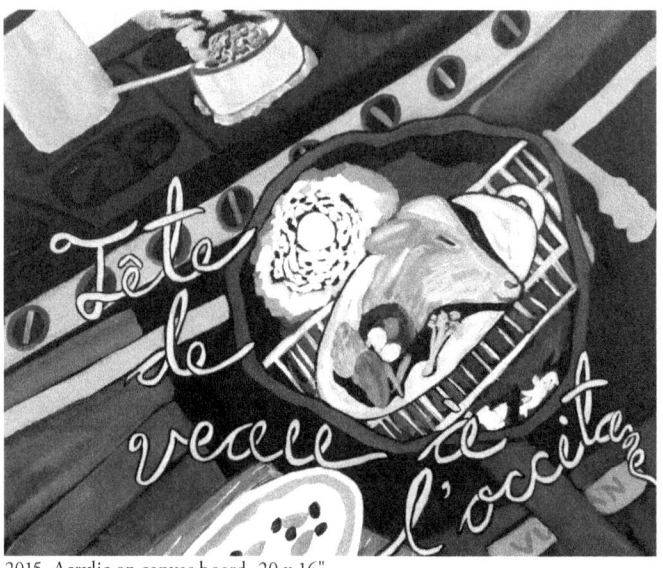

2015. Acrylic on canvas board, 20 x 16"

Calf's Head a lá Occitane and Those Tongs Are Too Short!

I am not a "foodie". I'm just an old cook who misses the trade sometimes. For one thing, it paid. Yet it also taught. Every day. Especially when the vodka pickled restaurant owner allowed you total experimentation during the slow time. An education with the added bonus of an hourly wage. I have been out of the business for several years, and can look back on its teachings fondly. Now, as everyone knows, you must boil the calf's head. Yet in the painting I have it roasting. Ha, not entirely true! I simmered it on low to be sure, and also the brain and tongue, for two hours with a mire-poix, and added a mainly tarragon bouquet garni, to maintain a happily scented kitchen while I prepared dessert. After straining the head, I rubbed it (also brain and tongue) with butter and salt and set it in the stove to rest while I arranged a platter of tomatoes, olives and hard boiled eggs.

It would have been a delicious entree, had I ever cooked a calf's head before. Come to think of it, this painting could serve as reminder to vegans and vegetarians alike that eating a cow's head today is probably one of the most disgusting unnecessary culinary wastes to earth and its systems, second only to shark fin soup served at nearly every table on holiday.

However, to me, its history is magical, thanks to the miracle of aging with its staple herb and spice, *memory and nostalgia*. A farmer Frenchman knew the calf personally, or at least the farm where it was born and partially raised. Even the Paris chef of 1875 had his connection to the countryside. I cannot imagine what truckloads of unpoetry are graduating today from our American culinary schools, nor the tourist trap Carnival Cruise ships where they intern just 2 years after developing rudimentary knife skills. Certainly the numbers are unsustainable. All at once, so many toilets flushing calf's heads into the sea, when just a few hours before, the tall chef hat server boy with some rehearsed éclat, flashed a psychotic smile for the army of iPhones clicking.

I am no foodie. Still, I can open *Larousse Gastronomique* to any page, and melt.

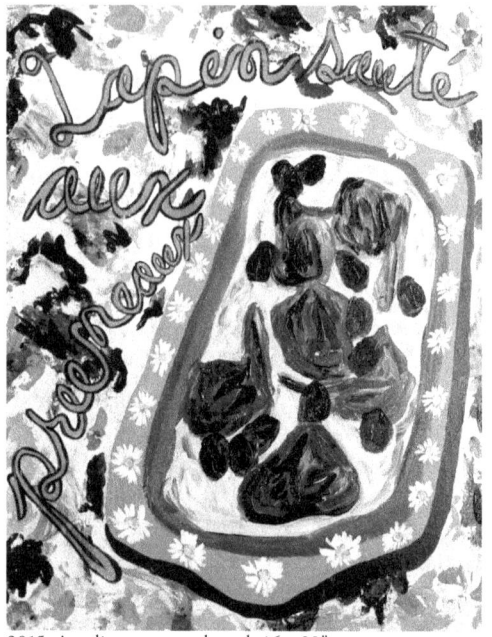
2015. Acrylic on canvas board, 16 x 20"

Rabbit Sautéed With Prunes

I'll probably live a lifetime never eating a rabbit. The species is very relieved that its women don't lay marbled-sized eggs or bigger. And so few people in my neighborhood make time to plant a lettuce patch. Mr. McGregor, the curmudgeon, smells like stale pipe tobacco, and lord knows he hasn't scrubbed his garden trousers in a month. Lagomorphs can smell his breed coming from a mile away.

If I won't cook a rabbit, I can still dream it. The colors of the old paper in the French parlor are pasted in my memory of a past that happened to other people. I was born on a French farm in 1893. Which reminds me of an old poem I wrote back when I was a wannabe French chef in a rinky-dink baked potato and cocaine waitress restaurant.

My Son Came Home With A Grimace So I Killed His Surprise Puppy

Outside of Arles, France, 1906

Ah Pierre my good boy!
It's dusk and you brought me our axle, no?
Yes father
Saul said no charge
for a bag of beans at harvest.
Here Pierre have some bread
I have a surprise for you.
No thank you father
I'm not hungry.
What's that?
My son, you've traveled all morning
over our land and Phillipe's too,
through the Black Forest
and on the plateau,
down into the valley
Fifty kilometers will make a man hungry!
Yes father, I know
but I bought a Big Mac and for two extra francs
got this nifty stuffed Grimace
It's big and purple and says
"comment allez-vous" when you pull on its ear.

Where are you going Papa?
Oh a puppy!
Father please no! Not that!

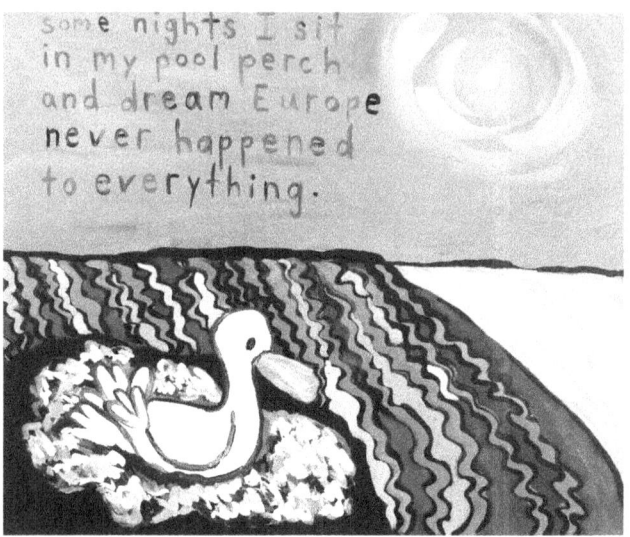

Some Nights I Sit in My Pool Perch and Dream Europe Never Happened To Everything 2015. Acrylic on canvas, 20 x 16"

Calling Paris, You Have Four Years

I am interested in working with French gallerists who would allow some attic space for me and my wife in 2019. Just room, maybe board, and available wall space in blanc to show the wealthy cosmopolite who stops by to inquire about art and artist. I am in earnest.

All France is welcome to apply for my residency, but Paris would be lovely. I feel in my heart that it would offer more respect for my Oster® blender ego than Anytown U.S.A. and its ever-present garage sale where I hang my latest work (to color the wall above the rusty mattock which I thought was a pick-ax). Got schooled again! This time by a dog lover. He dug a hole by hand once too, to bury his recently deceased mastiff. He didn't use a mattock, duh! The soil wasn't *that* hard. A pick ax was sufficient tool for seven feet down and a dead dog slightly larger than an overweight Walmart people greeter.

The garage sale was a huge success. Almost three hundred dollars for knick-knacks mostly, which also included fifty cents for a 30-year old pail of sand! The art—recent, colorful, expressive—hung beside the garlic and onions, glazed over by all eyes quicker than the children's educational books and toys. Not even a "Who painted that?", or "Did you actually write all these books?" Even the retired English professor next door showed no interest at all—not one glance at the Henry Miller book I was reading. An original London publication to boot!

Pardon my French France, but in this current state of disunion, we adhere to one motto, and one motto only:

Money talks. Bull shit gets bought.

Please visit my private, paid for website, and begin making offers to your lovely attics. Thank you.

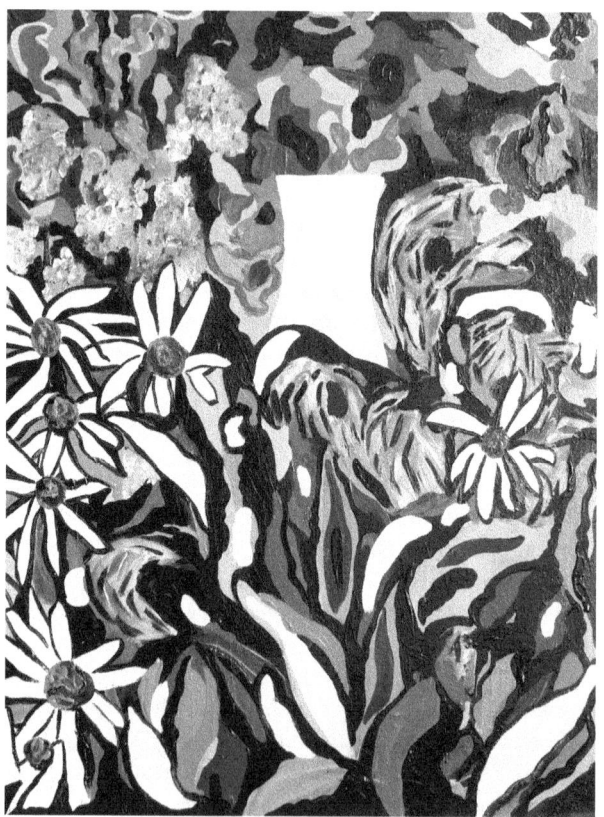

2015. Acrylic on canvas board, 16 x 20"

I Have Decided I Don't Want Nuclear Power It's 9:00 a.m.

Yup. I can declare it because I am an artist. I have determined that the atom is not ours to manipulate, so there—it's all settled. I am late middle-aged, a father, one day a grandfather, and an artist. Therefore I have more sway than the Grand Poobah of the military, the political hack, the parasitic corporate executive, the plumber with a dream... Why? Because I am a failure at collective thought, groupthink, mob rule, democracy and all isms leading towards extinction. I live between two industrial plants splitting the atom for more trucks and cars, and many McMansions where the atom-splitters dine on mediocre cooking. Ah yes, as artist, I am also a better cook than the atom-splitters and their ladder-up or ladder-down ilk. As artist, which is failure, I answer to myself and my love alone. Myself and my love alone want nuclear technology to cease. All except for medical procedures that uncancer the children who suffer tumors for the "greatest generation's" psychotic fear of their own timidity towards men in lab coats. Back in 1958, instead of "ducking and covering", little Teddy's grandparents should have been disjointing the joint chiefs of staff.

No worries. Myself as artist has matured, and declared the end of the nuclear age.

Time to plug into the sun because I say so.

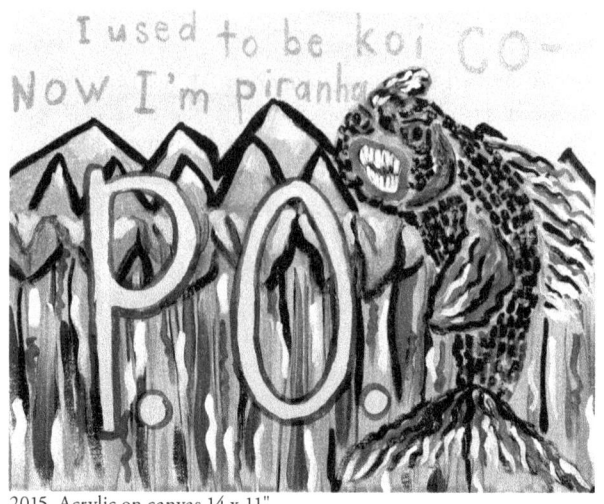

2015. Acrylic on canvas,14 x 11"

I Used To Be Koi CO—Now I'm Piranha P.O.

And neither koi nor piranha ever wanted to swim in Colorado! Arsenic and lead, no more algebraic equations in the head. No more thinking fish. Just like social studies class, we have dumbed down all species good and proper. Heavy metals to pass through the gills, settle in the soft tissue. Thank you non medical college degrees! Thank you too the "human good of the world", which seems to most times include huge sums of money somewhere, and another species' breaking back. Last week was benzene seepage, on Tuesday radiation, by Halloween, a thirteen-month gestation, and all little Frankensteins born heretofore pour mercury on their sugar cereal to promote bone growth. Why not? It's all topsy-turvy. Pollute a river, but if you're the law, why fine yourself? Alter life in a Gulf of Mexico, and if you're not the law, yet often have dinner with it, then forgo all Mississippi county jails for a lifetime of pleasure sailing. The yacht captain and crew have been to college too. They know all about the weather and the sea, and watch

FOX TV. So each share the same opinion as, let's say, a billionaire octogenarian. Believe in miracles, hope for the best, and be in the know that if you hate water pollution, it will hate you more, and continue its spilling laughter at the faces of your children. We the unmade never learned how to properly mob up and swipe a pipe at the knees of power and greed. The facade can only last as long as our brains get scrubbed by money. Bad people don't want money as much as they need you to starve for it. Why wait for the President to declare it, government radio releases the state of the union every hour on the hour. The Dow Jone's Industrial Average determines our economic vitality and whether or not we can count on Fruit Loops® this season. Each weekday we hear the numbers, even after news of the Keystone spill in Lincoln that stopped all traffic due to slippery conditions, as an army of moaning children projectile vomit black gold across highways and byways.

Oh well. What's next billionaire class? What can earth do for y'all? I sit writing between two nuclear power plants, waiting for a meltdown. I keep my lone iron pipe ready. You frackers have been here and gone, but will come back. Soon I imagine the fresh water police pushing us back at your behest. And the sad thing is—the super majority will let them. Rupert Murdoch told the banker who told the President (who was told by the general) that all drinking water gets poured individually into plastic baggies. A dime a drink. Then a quarter or a dollar—whatever the college grads can afford this year. No worries. Smartphone prices remain static. No matter what the illusion, information still travels top down while everyone pines for a carpeted automobile.

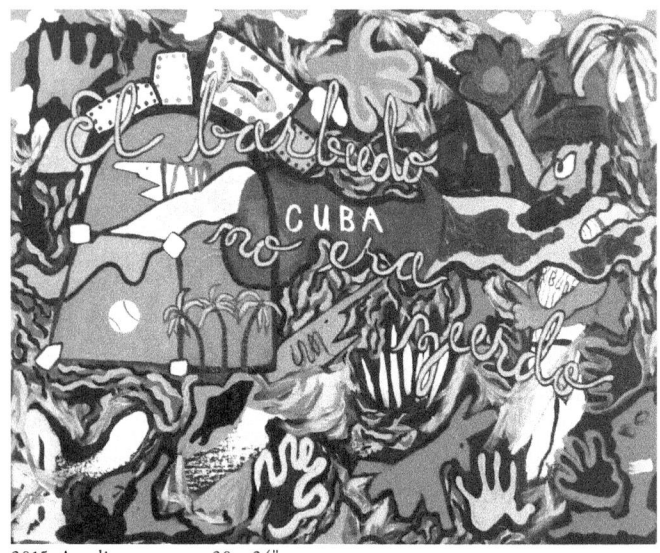

2015. Acrylic on canvas, 30 x 24"

Thank You Internet For Breaking the C.I.A.

For years I believed Fidel Castro tried out for The Washington Senators, failed, and evolved into the Cold War bat boy for the K.G. Bee-bees. A very popular children's American history book series said so, therefore it must have been true. I began to paint from my thought-dreams what I imagined a different outcome had Castro 3rd-stringed on the Senators. How dare this super jock take away my hopes to live out the rest of my days like an old man of the sea. Why didn't he try harder, go into coaching, teaching, anything but anti-J.P. Morgan socialism? Then I came upstairs to get the spellings right (when applying the permanence of paint I check every day spellings online, like "Washington"), and I discovered the truth. Fidel Castro was never a ball player. All the photos circulating the globe of him in a baseball uniform (Barbudos) was from just one game, a fund-raiser to keep the nation's triple A team financially stable. He was never scouted by professional baseball. Nor was he even left-handed, as the false history claimed (people of the 60's must have assumed that left-handed people leaned left in politics). Even the photo in the book show him wearing a glove on the left hand.

So I changed the painting midway through. I hope the Spanish translates, "The bearded one was not left-handed".

Let this serve as cautionary tale. If you believe in a C.I.A., and the good it makes of a world, then turn off all wired connections in the house, listen to NPR, watch government sponsored television like the PBS nightly news, have a scotch on Sunday afternoon, and allow high school history teachers to repeat the stories of their parent's childhoods. If, on the other hand, you wonder as free-born American why you are forbidden to travel 90 miles south of the border, connect to the Internet to discover a recent history of world lies. And please remember this, if you get anything from my painting... Knowledge is not power. In my experience, the people who know the most, tend toward aloneness. Power is maintained by control. And control is born of lies. Lots and lots of lies. So many lies.

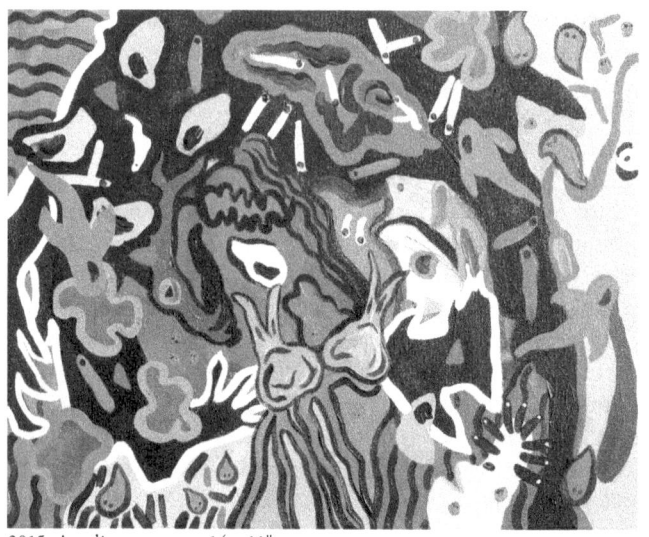

2015. Acrylic on canvas, 14 x 11"

Get This Algal Sludge Off Our Seas So We Can Import More Infantile Crap From China

Exclamation point.

Why not? It's enveloping our ships in sheet slime and slowing them down. I am so sick of progress impeded. Eradicate all producers of the ocean and save a penny on every dollar ordered from Sichuan Province. Sure, a few Chinese limbs will be lost to speed up production, but that is the price to pay for the latest American high school drop out to cash-in on bountiful ignorance at the dollar stores. The latter have multiplied like faux-happy Mormons all over rural New York State, serving up their first-of-the-month woe to the second-tier hapless victims of time poverty.

The control will always allow us sufficient nutriment to survive. The control knows it could not control without expired Little Debbies® or upstart potato chip companies made in New Jersey. Dollar foods fuel a bored, sloth-like purchasing urge for dollar picture frames, dog collars, scented candles, Santa hats, short-life batteries, greeting cards, children's books about Jonah and the whale, and pleather folders with auspicious insurance company logos.

And while basking in the dull light emanating from these exotic goodies, one can hear the latest made-in-a-high-rise country music hit—"I love America's militaristic waste of everything not Caucasian checkered tablecloth grandmother at the county fair".

The algae are practically acting like terrorists. As soon as that first green nasty pops its life-giving breath out from the arctic ice, I want a CENTCOM order to blow the North Pole to Pluto. Hell, let's act now. These ships must get through unimpeded. The Christmas season is nearly upon us. The Port of Shanghai is loaded and groaning with colorful, plastic manufactured things of jolly.

Killjoy algae! You're poised to destroy everything that makes my culture loathsome.

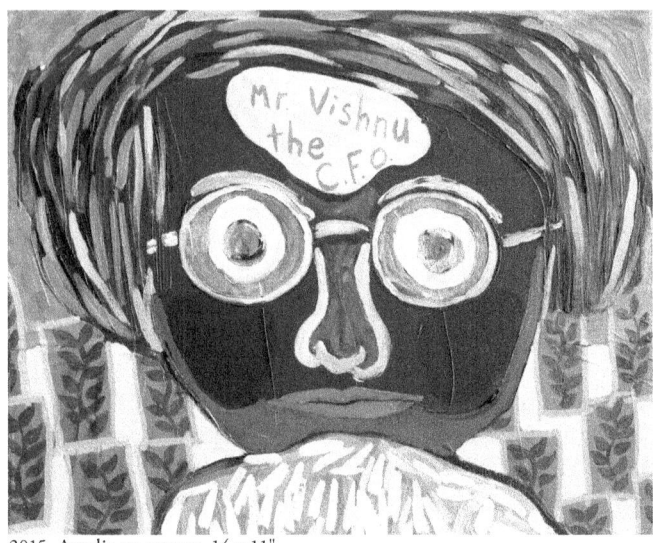

2015. Acrylic on canvas, 14 x 11"

Gandhi's Second Reincarnation

The first reincarnation as poor farmer's boy in Punjab ended in tragedy. Born a cretin from a heavily DDT overdosed mother, the once known "Great One", with new name "Dumbface", was pushed off a railroad bridge in 1989 by a gang of cruel village boys. Immediately he was born into a family of landlords in Goa living a charmed life educated in the finance of modern Hinduism. He was quite the studious hipster at business school, which earned him a fast-climbing position with Monsanto, and dreams of one day becoming the Lord companies' C.F.O. However, according to basic Vedic logic this will be impossible, owing to the fact that Mr. Vishnu is an Indian, and Monsanto hates Indians literally to death.

I hate Monsanto. But I was reborn politically correct in the U.S.A. That means it is "bad form" for justice seekers to voice disdain for bad people who create things and policies that are harmful to life.

Bt cotton˚ is not necessary for life nor dead cotton. Therefore, if just one Indian farmer cannot afford a bag of new suicide seeds in a crazy time when all of his "agriculturally correct" farmer neighbors tacitly agree to participate in their own culture's demise, and he commits suicide by drinking a gallon of Roundup˚, then Monsanto executives, lobbyists, politicians in pay, need to resign their positions immediately, or face BMW enemas administered at dawn.

Oh wait. I forgot. I live in a western industrialized oligarchy. What I meant to say was, "Live and let live Elvis says one shouldn't judge until you walked a day in the other guy's shoes people are all inherently good even the sinister ones who lick money like ice cream children on constant holiday".

There. I covered my righteous anger tracks for today. Now, back to work!

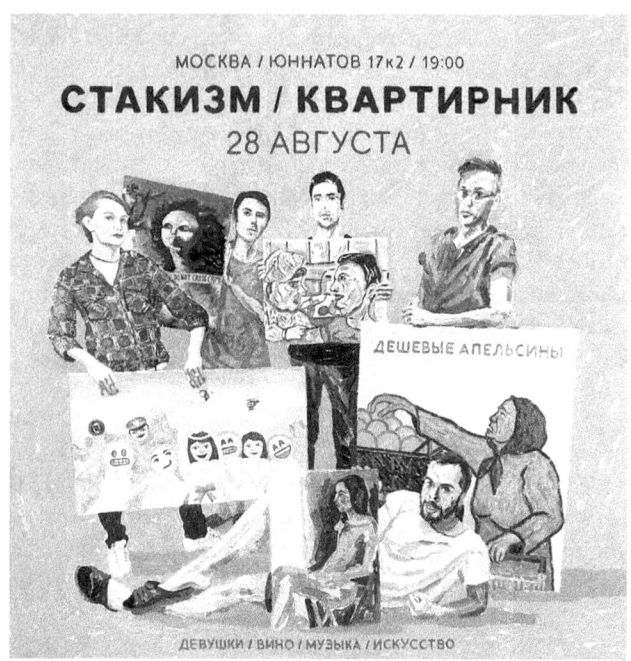

Moscow Stuckists of Supremeness.

In Russia They Know How Winter Can Ruin a Century

So summer is king.

I hope some of you can make it to Moscow on "the last Friday of leaving summer..." Below is the translation to the open invitation by a group of Stuckists in Moscow. They represent both the humility and triumph of painting so lacking in my country. Artists in New York City can learn a thing or two from this group of aficionados (I call them this with the highest respect). They post photos of their sessions. They learn together, drink together—plein air, cramped studio, critiquing each other with joy and enthusiasm. Shows in the woods, beside the canal, in the apartment. We Americans know nothing of painting camaraderie. Lonely business beggars locked down in the identity studio. I am so tired of existential art-think. Joy to the world! Thank you Russian painters!

Here is the Google translation to the invite above. Please go. I myself have been "corpsically" invited!

On the last Friday of leaving summer we invite you to our apartment exhibition: an event continues the tradition of the international movement Stuckism—in an informal family atmosphere, you can see the work of artists from the United States and Russia, to spend time in a friendly company, where the viewer and the artist closer than ever.

Art, music and wine sunset rays ... And yet—a small auction for those who want to go home with the painting under his arm;) and the lottery, one of the works—a gift to the winner ⌧

Friends, we wait for you on August 28 at 19:00 at the young naturalists - notes on the meeting page, contact us and come!

Participants:

Alexey Stepanov (Moscow / Saint-Petersburg)

Alena Levina (Moscow)

Andrey Makarov (Moscow)

Peter Generals (Moscow)

Michael Trubehin (Moscow)

Nikita Selyavina (Moscow)

Ilya Zelenetskii (St. Petersburg)

The corpse of Ron (Ron Throop) (Oswego, United States)

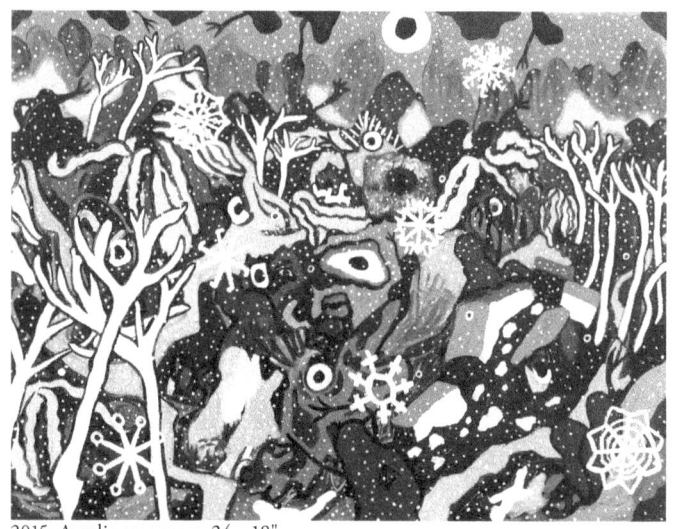

2015. Acrylic on canvas, 24 x 18"

This was Going to be a Criticism on the Cult of Personality, But Hell, I'm No Judge

Or, *Which China Snowflake is Wrong?*

I wanted to know more about Ai Weiwei, the Chinese thought-artist who spent some mid-eighties nights hanging out with Allen Ginsberg, the Time Magazine poet. Then some flycatcher bird with a tiny *Dharma Bums* tucked under the wing lit on my shoulder and told me to give neither my attention until I could count all the artists and poets in China who have raised children responsibly, and can do more than just "think up the next piece" to get paid. Omitting the choir, the disciples, the dumb college kid worshiping *Howl*, and the art history survey professor who can always make time for conceptual art, what value do their popular sermons bring to anyone on earth suffering from sensitivity overload? A dead Ginsberg and a live Weiwei knew how to tease an establishment class like the jesters in court who were consummate flatterers. They got "in" because they were jolly and non-threatening. They stayed in because their level of celebrity often payed for plane travel. If Weiwei truly loves China, he may think up art all day, anonymously, earning a very modest Chinese stipend, skimmed off the tippy-top of his investment banker portfolio. Ginsberg can run naked around phony hell for all I care. Neither have brought families closer together, stopped Fukishima, nor even dropped a flaming turd bag on Wall Street. No better than CEO's or soldiers careering for hollow relevance.

Ginsberg and Weiwei. Representatives of poetry and art to the great and glorious G-8. City mice at cheese play! Built to perpetuate confusion and circulate the funny money.

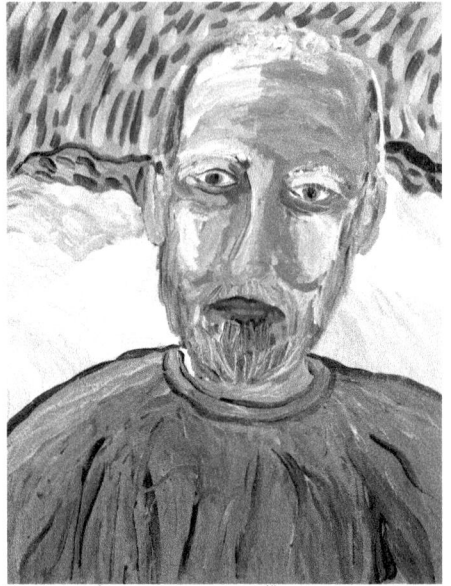

2015. Acrylic on canvas, 11 x 14"

Right-handed Study of My Left Face

I practically ran away from this one. I have painter's elbow pretty bad this month, and thought I would have a go this morning at right arm portrait painting. No mirror. Just memory of myself with beard and hair shirt. I don't suggest it to anyone. Like forcing unnecessary abdominal pain on a sunny day.

More On Russian Stuckism

Someone made an apple pie for the Moscow art party!

I also used to cook and bake tremendous amounts of food to satisfy the hungry hoard that I imagined would come to see a year's worth of Throop work. Soups, breads, cakes, cookies, quiches even. I remember my first public exhibition; I rented the space for a long weekend, designed and mailed 200 postcards, invited local media, spent hundreds of dollars on frames, and laid a veritable feast on several tables. I had a game where some lucky art lover could win an original Throop simply by answering correctly a trivia question. I never once considered it compensating for the inferior work on the walls. Rather, I naively thought, "this is how it's done". As artist, you warm your friends, family, and even some strangers with the human touch, and they give back by purchasing a painting, or, if that is out of any guest's price range, one of your several published books discounted on the table beside the free saved seeds. On the price list I included some barter ideas (still do), to get the conversation humming. On opening night, students from the college came at the behest of their professor, who was fast becoming a friend of mine. A few asked excellent questions, many showed serious interest. It was practically heaven while they eased in and out of the rented gallery. In the course of a weekend maybe up to five other unknowns came to view the work. One brought his elderly mother who really loved the food, and went so far to say that I should open up a catering business. Not a single word about the paintings! Even with several colorful titles like:

Veterinarian Ron Gets In Trouble With His Magical Time Machine

Welcome Suspicious Careerists

Don't Underestimate the Bite of the Toothless Dragon

Aut Libri, Aut Liberi (Either Books or Children)

All in all, it was still a wonderful experience. Truly a life-changing success. Likewise, a harbinger of future financial failures to come, but heck, it was an exhibition, not a stock speculation. An expressionist cannot help it if the laymen thinks television and a glass of wine the better night life to stimulate slumber. The dreams of the latter will amount to new carpet and cars. The expressionist as fool believes always in a better life. Often he or she must make one up to prove it.

These Russian painters are the future of art on earth. Their enthusiasm is more verve than the MoMA could squeeze from pathetic, uninteresting, uninspired bozos like the false clowns shown here:

Jesus, just look at them. No thought of exhibiting their innocence. They are prepaid for.

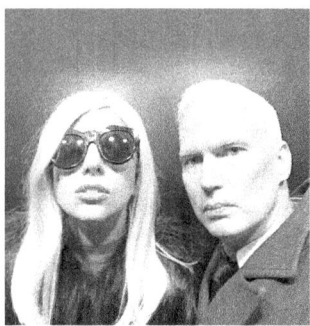

Lady Ga-ga and the anti-art bozo
Director of the MoMA

As to the constipated man in the photo, (the director of the MoMA), there is no doubt in my mind that he is oblivious to what makes art art. He would come to the Stuckist painting show, eat their food, chewing silently with no questions asked, and head back to the hotel with time to stream a few episodes of *Breaking Bad* through his iPad. Art-think must break away from this kind of power that doesn't even know what goes into an apple pie in order to bake it. There is art adventure out there. Seek it! Else fork over $25 to the MoMA to see what Bjork wears on a hot day.

Of course, many can partake in a revolutionary act. Attend the free art party to talk to human beings who help make talking to human beings a worth while pursuit.

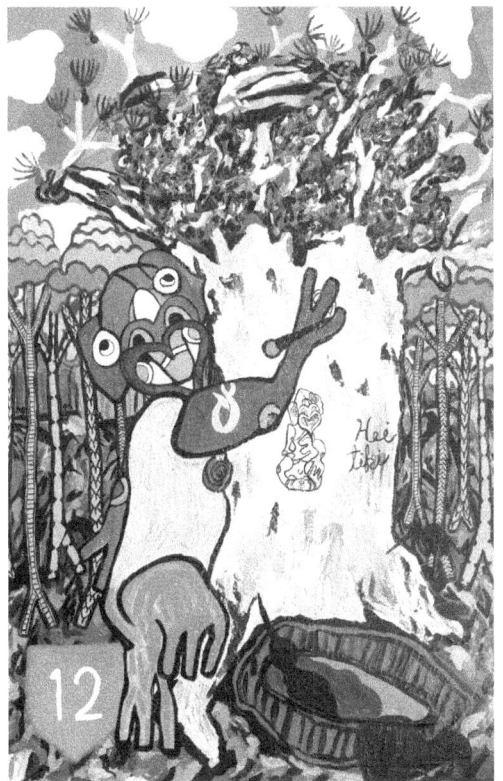

2015. Acrylic on canvas, 24 x 36"

Hei-tiki Parks Off State Highway 12

It's a Maori tiki of fertility carving into a kauri tree. I am looking forward to future grandchildren. It so happens my daughter and son-in-law (a Kiwi) are visiting the North Island this winter. Maybe they will run into Hei tiki.

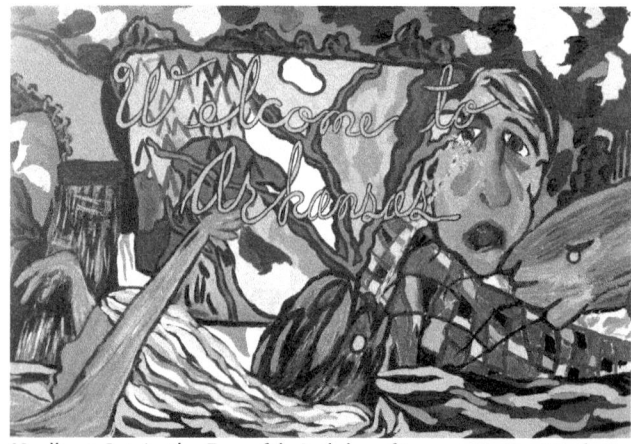

Noodling is Just Another Form of the Pathology of Love, or, *Cry You Non-loving, Noodling Rednecks... Cry!* 2015. Acrylic on canvas, 30 x 24"

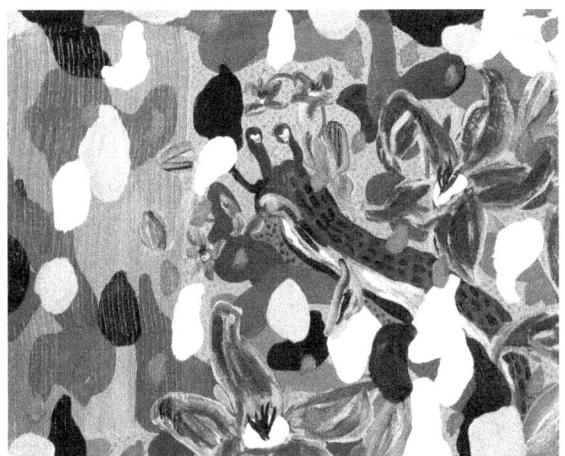

Hey Screed, Who Knew? You Can Hand Feed Borage to a Slug 2015. Acrylic on canvas, 14 x 11"

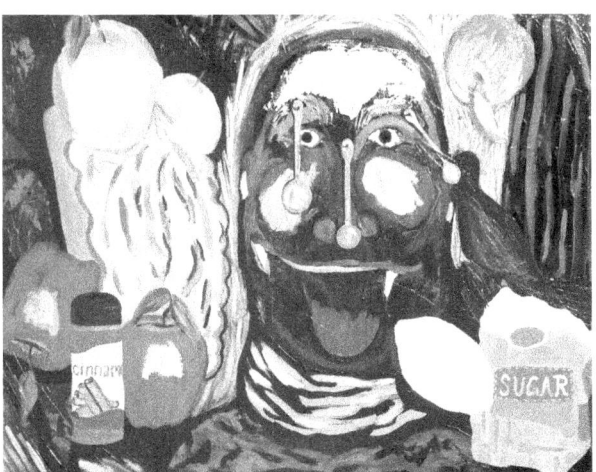

The Painter, The Glutton, and The Apple Pie 2015. Acrylic on canvas, 24 x 18"

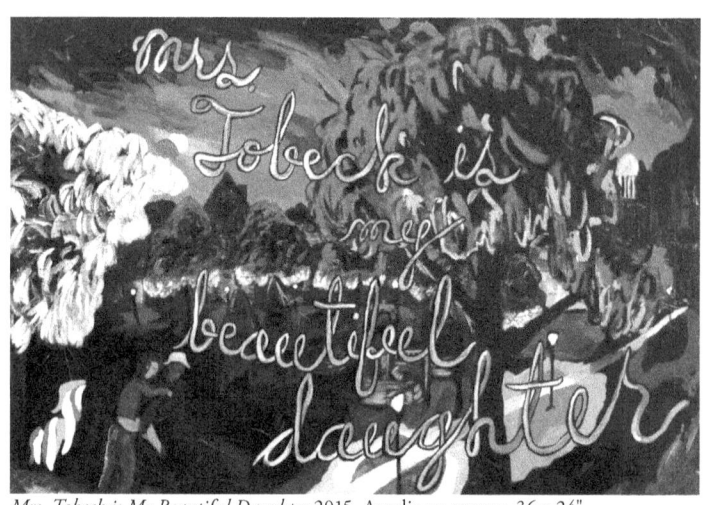

Mrs. Tobeck is My Beautiful Daughter 2015. Acrylic on canvas, 36 x 24"

Old Letter to Rose To Explain the Love of Life

Autumn is a time for little perfect memories of sheer bliss. Tonight I was a demon, you were a ghost, and together we buried a little witch under a pile of leaves. Perfect. I will never forget this happy memory! My job, my only true employment, is to think on these things. I am a lonely painter, pirate cook, and poetic imbecile all rolled up into one huge clog of hyper-sensitive neurons. That makes for worthwhile walks in harvest moonshine. Night walks with you talking about our memories and our plans.

Everything you are I have seen in me at the best of times. But I am not as constant as you. Nor can I compare to the stuff of you, like breasts and belly button. I do not sway hips to drive all the boys crazy with desire. No small of my back that cries "My God, press your thumbs into me!"

Rose, Rose, Rose... I never had a single soul to share my dreams. I am confident enough to believe in what I hope for. You say that you have a hard time trusting someone. Imagine Ron to be a maple tree. Now ask me, "Will you be here tomorrow?"

"Yes Rose, these roots go deep."

"You must fear something?"

"I have only one."

"Well?"

"I fear before bed you walk to the shed, and oil that chainsaw you use for a head."

"But I don't understand."

"I guess, Rose, that you'd have to be a tree to understand."

The moral of this dialogue: When a tree says he loves you, quit your job at the lumber yard if the feeling's mutual.

Food gets the last picto-word:

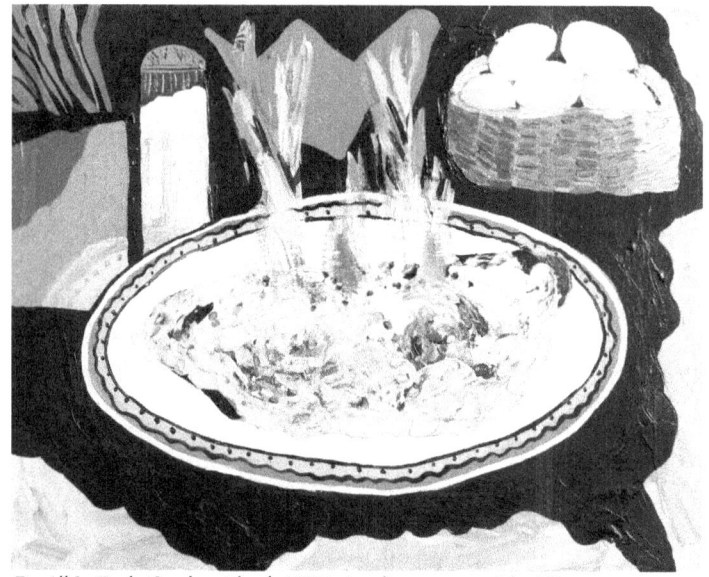

For All Its Faults Omelette Flambeé 2015. Acrylic on canvas, 14 x 11"

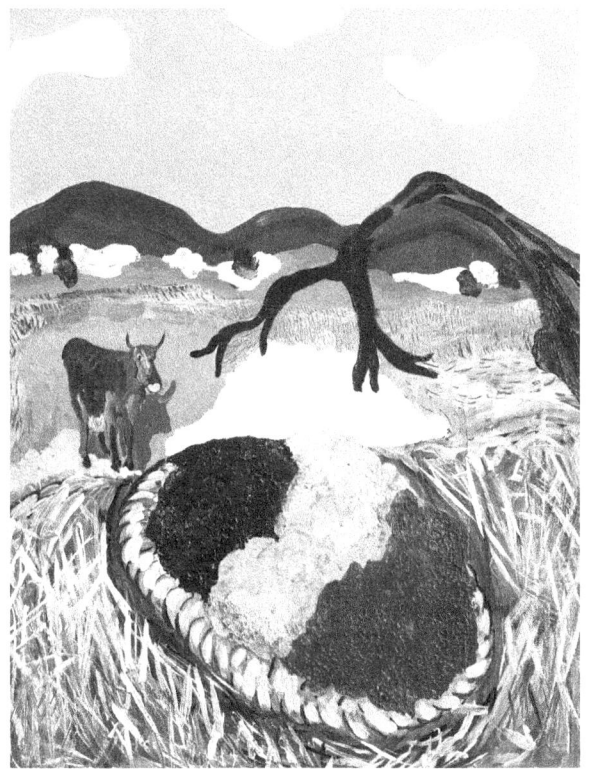

Blackcurrants, Whitecurrants, Redcurrants Disprove Existentialism
2015. Acrylic on canvas, 11 x 14"